Sand

By Eric Marley

With gratitude to:

Jeb Barton
Hermann Hesse
Derrick Jensen
Fred Wolf
Mrs. Hippie, Mrs. Spelbrink and Mrs. Forster
The "Seth" study crew
Dr. Ken Stikkers
Eckhart Tolle
Pema Chodron
Danielle Mercurio
Jeff and Christine Walter
Eric Pritchard
Thomas Isom
Kari Morton
April Theisen
Red Road communities way past, past and present
Friends that encouraged me and early editors
Facebook acquaintances and others that encouraged me –
(please forgive glaring omissions)!

I especially wish to thank my parents who, like our old banty
hen that couldn't quite understand why her duckling chicks
loved the water, accept me as best they can.

Table of Contents

Foreword

"There is no greater disaster in the spiritual life than to be immersed in unreality… when our life feeds on unreality, it must starve. It must therefore die."- Thomas Merton, 1915-1968

"There is no such thing as a way or ways of consciousness; individual ways turn up merely by virtue of consciousness making itself understood." - Longchempa

At first glance, these two statements appear to contradict one another. One statement implies that it is incumbent upon us to know "reality" and the other says there is no set way of consciousness, meaning there is no one correct way to experience "reality". Both these men are revered thinkers within their spiritual traditions and lived often solitary existences, albeit many centuries apart. Longchempa was an important Buddhist teacher that lived in central Tibet in the 1300's, while Thomas Merton was a Trappist monk that lived late in the past century.

What is interesting to me is that in addition to being a Catholic might fall, from many traditions, as long as it did not offend the innate sensibilities of our individual spirits. Suspected truth discovered from this point of view would also almost necessarily retain the same fluid quality as the attitude which birthed it, leaving the learner to hold to what seems true at the time while being open to being taught from whatever worthy Source is able to teach us as we progress through life. This would include

4

higher truths that we are increasingly ready to apply, even though they may seem to contradict "true" ideas we once held.

Of course, there are teachers with impure motives in this world, so a spirit of discernment is needed by the potential student about what messages can be trusted and, maybe more importantly, how the newly revealed truth should be applied in this existence. In "Sand", the idea is presented that true concepts themselves should be our teachers. Only Truth herself knows what the student is ready to hear and implement in their lives. It is therefore incumbent upon the student to place himself in a position to be taught; in a place of humility, play and exploration, including exploration of ideas once held inviolable.

Approaching life and truth in this manner will, I suspect, put our wandering souls increasingly in touch with increasingly pure truth, and insulate us from that which distracts us from the peace that is the nature of our eternal souls.

May we find our truths from that place, and may we seek as humble children of a loving Creator to find commonalities rather than divisions in whatever we choose to call reality, or the way of consciousness.

--Eric Marley, December 2013

Preface

What you are about to read is an account of a conversation that occurred in a dream I had not long ago after a challenging day. The conversation wasn't too long, but it has infused my life ever since. It's as if all the colors that meet my eyes have been changed. The whole world looks new, lit from its very energetic vibrations, physically brighter, substantially deeper, like seeing things in three dimensions for the first time. And, where once I had seen mostly decay and immorality, dishonesty and bad luck, I now see the Earth and life, Life, as something entirely new. The difficulties remain, but there is an undercurrent I had forgotten existed.

Another result of the experience of the dream is that everything now seems to move too quickly, as if Western culture simply wants to prove how fast it can go without regard for anything but the speed it can generate. Even though I am in it too, it feels like it did when I as a teenaged young man would rev my car beyond its capability. At first, the engine would respond with greater speed, but the increase in speed would eventually taper. The increasing noise of the screaming engine would not translate to a corresponding increase in speed. It was less of a roar and more of a complaint. When this occurred, it was time to shift. I think the same thing must be said of our culture.

The enlightening effect of the dream was matched by my frustration while trying to communicate not only the events within it but the meaning of the concepts that were presented. Indeed, it became known to me in the course of the dream that not only was I under no obligation to tell anyone anything about it, but to do so may well harm the hearer in some way.

The reasons for this were two-fold.

First, spoken language is not appropriate to use when communicating certain concepts. It is simply too much to ask of the language. The words are not there. Of course, the concepts can be approached on some level. But care should be exercised; for I came to understand that the desire to discuss these things may well be more a function of my own egoic needs rather than a genuine concern for a fellow traveler. Each human is in the midst of their own walk and, in a very real sense, their own world.

It's true that concepts relating to the Unseen can and should be spoken about. But a significant problem occurs when we consider the far-reaching impact that even seemingly insignificant Truths can have on our being. After all, they pertain to an existence that is literally infinitely larger than that which we mortals experience. Therefore, deep sensitivity should be used in discussions pertaining to these keys because we don't know their power, nor can we truly conceive their power. The effect of these on the soul can be enlightening, and we hope it is. But truth can also be devastating to the soul's awakening or rather, the mortal's "remembering" on some level their true nature.

Sometimes we are just not ready to hear, and that's ok.

In the end, it should be the Concept itself that informs the student, not a fellow mortal. The Concept can search the student and show only that amount that informs in a healthful way. Since this is the case, far more emphasis than is currently given should be placed on preparing the hearer to receive whatever concept they're prepared to hear, rather than foisting a preconceived curriculum upon the student, established by one that is supposedly further along the path. In the end, a type of spiritual anarchy is what serves mankind best.[1]

---

[1] 1 Corinthians 3:2. In this Biblical verse, Paul is speaking about doctrinal "milk before meat". The concept has to do with the hearer being prepared to understand concepts hitherto unknown. The point is that only the concepts themselves thoroughly "know" the level of preparation of the student.

Finally, a few notes about:

- Punctuation: I've capitalized words and phrases that have to do with the realm of consciousness. The title "earth" for example, if referring to the planet as a sentient being, is spelled "Earth". If I were referencing dirt, the spelling would be in the lower case. The language she speaks is called the "Language", since it exists with or without humankind, or even mortality. The title "Intelligence" is another example. As the most basic form of connection to All That Is (or "God"), it is capitalized. If the word were being used in reference to someone's intellect, it would be "intelligence".
- Science: Particularly at the end, I can think of no science that would remotely agree with the final scene. But this is not meant to be a treatise on science. The events described are used only to point to the author's view of the enormity of Life.
- Footnotes and Endnotes: No need to get too serious about this topic, although it's worth an investment in time to look at it. Some of the footnotes are there to bring additional thoughts to the subject and some are my attempts at interjecting humor. The endnotes usually provide more substantive commentary.
- God: This is a word that is so charged with pre-conceived concepts that I rarely use it. The terms "All

That Is" or "Creator" are generally used instead, but they mean basically the same thing. "Creator" is meant to mean several different roles and is purposefully left vaguely defined, as are the terms "Oversoul" and "Being".

- Tangerine Dream: The concept for "Sand" came to me while driving through a mountain pass towards Bend, Oregon where I live. I was listening to a track called, "Hyperborea," after the TD album of the same name, and I became astounded by the enormity of Life. In order to give the reader a "soundtrack" of sorts for a specific part of the story, I marked in the footnotes where to start the music, if one were to find the track and read along. *The idea is to create a kind of a guided meditation for a specific and important part of the story.*

- Religion: I am not against religion. I see much good that comes from adherence to a set of dogma to the exclusion of others, particularly when it comes to developing healthy habits and ways of being. I suspect, however, that many adherents to religious orders get caught up in practices and dogma to the exclusion of the reasons behind them, to their own detriment. This alone does not make religion itself undesirable, any more than a signpost warning of a windy road ahead might make to a driver in a dark night. The road still has value, and the sign itself doesn't make the road impassible. It might, however, be best to take it a little slower.

A stickier situation demanding more attention occurs when people are "called" to lead others. For both the leader and the followers, great care should be taken so neither are deceived, the original communications are preserved and/or conditions are created such that the followers themselves can enjoy the message as close to the great Source as possible. All this, while acknowledging that Truths themselves teach far more effectively and efficiently than mankind, no matter how inspired.

It's a tall order.

Sand

The emptiness in my heart held constellations. It had been a day of disappointment compounded exponentially. All the teachings of Jesus, the Buddah, Krishna, Lao Tzu and Sitting Bull wrapped the emptiness but could not penetrate it. Instead my heart stood still; a lonely star in a distant and cold galaxy.

I sat on my bed for 30 minutes in my work clothes, mulling the day. A coolness lay untouched just under my skin. I didn't have the strength to get out of my clothes, brush my teeth, meditate and crawl into bed in a more peaceful manner as was my normal routine. I knew somewhere in my soul's void that peace would have knocked quietly and then filled the space, had I capitulated. After all, many times I had felt despair, and many times I had forced myself to assume this position of humility and self-compassion, clearing the chorus of criticism in my own mind. I knew that if I went through the motions, however begrudgingly, the beastlike beings would quiet before the majesty of light that would infuse itself into every dark corner of my inner being.

But tonight the cruel coolness dampened any light. My star stood eternally alone.

I swung my feet on the bed and kicked off my shoes. I didn't get under the covers. I lay there, looking for patterns in the texture on the ceiling, and in the texture of my life, but was unable to find any at all.

At the front of my skull, my brain began to shut down. A fatigue that seemed to murder every cell it touched hit my eyes as they closed. The last thing I remember was my body sinking further into the bed. The bedspread rose over my body like water.

My eyes shot wide. His face was just fading, like when one looks at a bright light too long and then, looking away, the negative light obscures one's vision for a moment. The last things to fade were his eyes; eyes that were twin suns made of something that felt like my childhood, a time of freedom and play, joy, newness, laughter – an essence that seemed to recall a hummingbird (but I didn't yet know why). The two suns eventually faded and I was left to look in wonder at my ceiling with no patterns.

But something remained.

I leapt from my bed of nails with the newness of a spring bud just breaking the earth. I needed to write what I could before any of it faded. Literally running to my desk, I skidded, nearly falling. This produced a spontaneous, joyous giggle, seemingly plumbed from the same depths that had produced such agonizing despair only…minutes? hours? eternities? before. But they weren't the same depths at all. The giggle was borne of eternity, of a "cool and star-bright laughter"[2], as Hermann Hesse put it, while the despair was decidedly of this mortality with its assumed disease and illness. No matter what, it was certainly the same day, or early the next, that I had lain down sick and nearly suicidal. What a difference a dream makes.

The Dream[3]

In my dream, I was walking on endless dunes, and I had been doing that for a long time. Shade was nonexistent, almost as if it were a planet made of nothing but sand. There were no trees in existence, not a blade of anything that looked like grass, no lichen, no rock; only ankle-deep sand. My walk was labored. I saw my face, sunburned, peeling in white strips in places, exposing red skin that looked like it could never heal. I had a towel over my head to protect my brain from sunstroke. This was futile because the towel itself was nearly ablaze, making my

---

[2] "Steppenwolf", by Hermann Hesse. Hesse understood and could illustrate concepts without damning the souls of his readers. On a personal note, I've read that book dozens of times now. I get something new that pertains to my life every time.
[3] If you are following along with Tangerine Dream's "Hyperborea," start the track now.

head feel like it was in an oven. I wore some type of white tunic. I remember thinking with some irony that I was glad it was white and not some dark color, but it didn't really matter. I was dying from the inside out from thirst more than anything else. My throat was closing with multiplying scars inside it. Every breath brought burning air past my infernally dry mouth into my hesitant lungs, scorching them as well. Even my teeth felt hot.

But worst of all were my feet. As I was somehow barefoot in this inferno, they were nearly the color of blood. I had long since stopped looking down at them for fear that I would watch one lift out of the sand to take a step and it would simply detach or come up black. The sky was that kind, inviting blue that is the favorite of children. To me, it looked only like water. But instead of the color of a cool, life-saving stream, it was the color of a beautiful but undrinkable, briny ocean.

As I watched myself trudge through the sand, I realized that this poor lost soul (from here on, The Wanderer) was indeed searching for water, and my observing dreaming self (the Dreamer) knew that it was nearby. The Wanderer might well miss it, but the Dreamer could see it. It was there.

The Dreamer's eyes began to burn with tears from shear empathy. "Please," he said aloud to The Wanderer, "turn just to the south. It's there."

To the Dreamer's surprise, the lonely Wanderer stopped as if he had heard something very faint, very still; a breath almost, less than a whisper. He looked up at the sky towards the cruel, determined sun, and then to the south. He frowned. He seemed to be considering something. There was a steep dune in the distance that stretched to the east and west for maybe a mile before diving back into the featureless desert.

He had nothing to lose.

[4]Using the sun as a marker, The Wanderer began his labored walk south. When he reached the bottom of the incline, he looked at it with the eyes of one facing the method of his own death; the charging grizzly, the rogue wave, the car sliding sideways toward the careening truck. I saw his knees begin to buckle and his lower lip begin to tremble. But incredibly, just as suddenly I, The Dreamer, saw new strength – maybe his last – still both his lip and his knees. His eyes turned hard and determined and, with the purposeful gait of a man walking to a gunfight, he started up the hill. I somehow felt proud of this supremely suffering man for moving onward at all.

---

[4] If you're listening to Hyperborea, this part corresponds roughly to 2 minutes, 37 seconds (2:37).

Slipping, at times seeming to slide a foot backwards for every step forward, he labored up the hill. His breathing both intensified and decreased in efficiency. I could tell that his body was shutting down. I began to think in terror that he might not make it to the top of the hill. He doubled over and swayed. He wanted to cry, but he simply had no strength. He was ready to succumb, to tumble to the bottom of the hill, to let his body mummify and be consumed by the eternal white sands.

Would it be that bad?

But then, with a great show of will, I saw the weary, worn Wanderer look upward to the top of the hill. It was within reach. With renewed courage and the very last of his reserves he struggled and stumbled to the top.

He stopped. It was rock.

Oddly, the rock was blood red, stretching straight out like a carpet in front of him. He had never seen this color in the desert, but in his bewildered state he asked no lasting questions. One thing for certain: there was no water in this place. He could see what appeared to be a cliff directly ahead, its edge maybe a hundred meters away. Aside from that, heat waves, not rippling waters, burned though his eyes and hopes.

He frowned as he doubled over, putting his hands on his knees, trying to recover his breath. I saw him look at the sky with searing anger as red hot as the rock in front of him.

He yelled to the sky with all the rage that had built within him, "Why did I waste the last of my strength to come here to die? I could have done that in the dunes! My intuition is worthless, and so are you!"

Sobs wormed their way up to the throat of the man, only to be choked back by anger more intense than his sorrow or disappointment. The thought occurred to him that he could throw himself off the cliff. After all, he *was* standing on rock. Maybe the deep red tint of the rock meant that it was to be a place of his death, a divine sign. And maybe this was not the only rock in this eternal desert. Maybe it ended in a sheer cliff with a jumble of compassionate stones below that would mercifully remove the little life force that was left in him. It was this thought that now gave him resolve.

He walked forward with the halting, hollow step of a man walking to the gallows.

Suddenly, as if he had been slapped, his eyes sprung open wide. A cool breeze. To you and I the heat would have been searing, but to him it was cool in contrast to what he had experienced in the shapeless sand under the apathetic blue eternity above.

"No," he thought, "please..." as he moved forward.

First a thin blue line bounced up into his vision. Another step made the line thicker, and then thicker. Ten steps after he had first seen the blue line, the man stood on the edge of a precipice maybe 30 feet high. There were rocks below, but they were part of a sheer cliff that stretched away under water bluer in many gradients than any sky, turning the submerged red stones into a delicious eggplant purple.

[5]A single tear from what seemed like the last molecules of moisture in his body started down his cheek before being slurped greedily by the resolute, angry sun and his moisture-starved skin.

[6]His tunic and towel fell to the rock at his feet. The Wanderers eyes were new. He stood at the precipice, feeling cooler air than he could ever remember feeling come up from the lake and caress his body as a lover. The air was medicine - a body and soul salve. The water would be even more so.

---

[5] Hyperborea, 3:48
[6] Hyperborea, 4:02

Naked now, he took two steps forward and with form that would make a competitive diver jealous, he arched his back and spread his arms as an eagle spreads her wings. Seemingly suspended by the heat, by all his pain and hope, he paused in mid-air before starting down with increasing speed.

The air on his skin felt warm, but it cooled him nonetheless as he fell. However, it was nothing compared to the water.

[7]And then...

Pressure felt on the crown of his head ears muffled with the sound of water rushing into them eyes burning not unpleasantly as he opened them to see nothing but blurry blue.

But what he noticed more than anything was the pain in his feet diminishing by the instant. Rising the last few feet to the air above, he opened his mouth to allow the coolness to flow into it, the first he had felt in as long as he could remember. Refreshing water caressed his teeth and the inside of his mouth. Slurping gratefully, he urged it past his swollen throat. Nothing

---

[7] Final Hyperborea marker: 4:15. See him swimming effortlessly away...

had ever been sweeter. He smiled a sigh, and then laughed with joy.

The sky no longer seemed like the enemy it had been. He turned on his back and, turning his head as he backstroked, surveyed the lake in which he swam. It was a perfect circle, framed by sandstone cliffs.

Oh, no! Cliffs!

A terrifying thought came to him: what if there was no way out of the lake? What if it was all framed by sheer cliffs? Could the Universe be that cruel, to give a man dying of thirst a lake that would only drown him? Given his brutal wanderings, he had no comforting answer for that question. He turned over from backstroking in terror to look in the direction he had been swimming, for to this point there was little in his memory that gave him any indication of enduring Universal mercy.

But there it was.

In fact, there was only one way out of the lake. It appeared to be directly ahead of him, maybe a quarter mile from where he effortlessly kicked at the present moment. Moreover, there seemed to be a small stand of trees at the same site.

Trees!

Noting the distance, it occurred to him that he should be in no shape to swim even the distance from his present location to the bank, let alone that he had swum a fair distance in addition to it. But the water seemed not only to buoy him without effort on his part, but to be pushing him along towards the lake's exit.

He looked back and, to his monumental surprise, the cliff from which he had jumped was far in the distance. He could barely make out the place from which he had launched, now only what appeared to be a distant red rock fall, the only one like it in his sight. Somehow, he had swum the vast majority from the cliff to the bank without even knowing it. His body still felt depleted, but there was a type of electricity flowing through it that felt of vitality, healing and the beginnings of deep health.

The Wanderer looked back towards the edge of the lake in the direction he had been swimming, put his head down and started stroking towards shore. His strength had mysteriously returned and even increased.

Now The Wanderer stood waist-deep in the water and began to walk out from his swim, naked as before. His body hummed with life. He hadn't felt this energetic since his youth, far in the past. In front of him was a lush, well-kept oasis. At the base of the first tree was a small bundle of cloth, tied with a red silk sash. He approached it, sensing somehow it was meant for him.

Untying the sash, he unfolded a tunic of fine cotton. He slipped it on, wincing out of sheer habit from anticipation of the pain of cloth against his burned skin, but there was none. With a relieved smile and laugh he tied the tunic with the red sash and looked at the miracle around him.

Within a few moments he had walked to and was standing under the first shade he could remember experiencing. It was a tree that was not indigenous to the area – none were - but he was not arguing. He plucked a ripe mango and tore into the pregnant orange flesh. Sweet, sugar-laden juice flowed down his skin which seemed to take nourishment from it as well. Looking around, he saw papaya, lemon, almond, fig and guava trees. Spinach, dandelions and an asparagus-like flower grew in clumps nearby. Each of these lost a small fraction of its persistent production to the starving man.

The Wanderer noticed some other kinds of life around him. Flowers buzzed with bees, and a hummingbird especially drew his attention. He had always loved hummingbirds, had had a natural inexplicable affinity for them. He watched in awe as one raced about from flower to flower, and he found himself face to face with another that appeared to be... it was too odd to even think... smiling at him. He tentatively smiled back, and the tiny bird sped away.

The Wanderer was suddenly exhausted. His belly full of water, nuts, fruit and vegetables, he laid his body on cool, wet sand on the shore of the savior lake. His eyes were shaded by leaved limbs that fanned him and the man slept for what seemed like a month.

When he awoke, there was another man in front of him.

To say this was a man, however, is to give the moniker far too much credit. The term "Being" was far more appropriate and will be used henceforth, although it is still insufficient. The Wanderer had never seen anything in all of creation more beautiful than this. The Being radiated something that could only be called acceptance from every fiber of his body. But it also contained humor and a deep sense of playfulness mixed with fathomless wisdom. Even his clothing, which matched his except for a multicolored sash, radiated this message.

"Who are you?" The Wanderer whispered in wonder to The Being before him as he began to stand.

"I am your Oversoul,[8]" The Being replied. "I created this."

The Wanderer had never heard the term "Oversoul", but he was too taken with what he had told him about creating the oasis to ask. Instead he said reverently and with wonder, "You created

---

[8] The term "Oversoul" can mean many things. I will leave it up to the reader to interpret the final identity of this personage, but for our purposes at this point it is a very advanced spirit.

25

this little oasis? Let me assure you, sir, this has saved my life. I am forever in your debt." The Wanderer bowed humbly.

"Thank you," The Being said with humility that matched the others'. "But I mean I created it all."

The Wanderer's face lit up. "The lake, too?" he exclaimed in the deepest gratitude. "You can't imagine my feelings as the lake came into view after so long in the desert! You can't have any concept of what it meant to me to plunge into the lake itself, to drink the water, to swim in it. And look," The Wanderer said, pointing to his feet, "even my feet are healed. They don't hurt! The skin is all back to normal. How did you do that? Is this really healing water? I can't thank you enough!"

The Being smiled with an expression that one might give a child that is discovering a subject that has been just beyond its comprehension for as long as it has lived.

"I created the desert, too."

The Wanderer's face fell. Darkness like a thundercloud obscured the light of joy and thanksgiving in his eyes. Something akin to violence contracted his heart.

"How could you?" It was more an accusation than a question. "Do you know how much I suffered there? I suppose you made the sand, the heat, everything? I thought when I saw you that I felt... something... something that felt like love coming from you. But there's no way you could feel love and create what you did... I can't believe it."

The Being smiled with, if it were more possible, even more light than before.

"Come," he said gently, reaching out his hand.

As furious as The Wanderer had been, it was a mortal's furor and hence was no match for the love of the Being. He looked down and placed his hand in that of the Being's. The Wanderer looked up into his face and blinked.

In the split second that his eyes were closed, they had been transported somewhere.

They were standing on a cliff directly across from the one from which The Wanderer had jumped. He could see through the rippling heat the red stain that led from the top of the cliff from where he had jumped into the water. He knew it was the same place because there were no other red rocks to be seen. The Wanderer looked down the face of the precipice where they now stood and saw the small oasis below, where he had recently been happily napping.

He looked back up into the face of the Being, whose demeanor had changed slightly. His face seemed the same, but his eyes were no longer smiling with the intensity they had been.

"Why are you here?" The Being asked.

"How did you… I guess you brought us up here," The Wanderer answered, frowning. "Right?"

The Being's eyes softened slightly and a slight smile softened his mouth.

"Sometimes even I forget the way a Wanderer sees the world. Your view is generally limited to what you see at the time. Let me rephrase: why are you alive?"

The Wanderer thought of his life. He couldn't remember a time in his recent past that wasn't fraught with hunger, thirst, loneliness. He knew there had been a time when he was with people. He had lived in cities, traveled to distant lands, driven cars. It seemed as if he had had a family once. But these things were all recognized in an almost conceptual, dreamlike way. There were no specifics. All he had as a specific, recent reference was the pain of the desert and the relief of the lake and oasis. These seemed to have no clues as to the answer that The Being sought.

"I guess I don't know."

The Being nodded. "Yes, and it is acceptable that you do not know right now. You lack the perspective you need to truly understand. I am going to ask you to follow my instructions. If you do so, you will begin to begin, to begin to gain some tentative understanding, which will bring perspective. Will you do what I ask?"

The Wanderer nodded solemnly.

"OK then. Look into the lake."

He turned his gaze from the Being's eyes towards the lake far below.

Suddenly, the blueness of the lake filled his vision. The hue grew progressively darker until darkness was all he saw, as if he were many fathoms under the water, encased in cool, deep blue weightlessness. A light came, blinding. He saw around him stars and a sun appear, and then multiple stars and suns. He saw them live and die, comprehending their interactions. This comprehension filled his body as if with light. He smiled in wonder not only at the order but the aliveness that infused everything he saw.

Last of all he saw a new star, somehow recognizing it as familiar and homelike. It was the very sun that had recently tortured him so thoroughly in the desert. Only now it looked not only innocuous but made of a spiritual, even holy light he could not quite comprehend based on his recent experience.

Among the planets in its orbit, he saw a small red, spinning Earth, presumably the one upon which he stood. It was young and alive, now filling his vision as it drew nearer. As The Wanderer watched, enthralled, he felt the presence of The Being next to him. He was safe, secure. They stood together as the new Earth cooled and oceans formed.

The Being spoke in awe. "This is among my greatest creations. This is not only part of your reason, but part of mine."

"What do you mean?" The Wanderer asked.

"Take as much in with your eyes as much as you can, and let what you see inform your soul," was all he said in return.

At the explosion of a star traveling close to the new Earth they watched life begin upon it. Whether the life came from the star or if the star was merely a catalyst to awaken sleeping life upon the Earth was unimportant. They both watched in stillness as the new creations coagulated, multiplied, mutated, transmutated, bred and cross-bred. He saw individuals and species come into being, thrive and then die.

He comprehended that the Earth was a manifestation of the love of the Being, and that there was a common Language that was understood by all life on the Earth. It was not only conversational, it was instructional in a way that The Wanderer could never have imagined. To say the Earth spoke telepathically was the closest thing he could think of, but it was woefully short of being adequate. Moreover, the conversations he witnessed were less like separate entities communicating than a type of holy self-talk. Every interaction was an illustration of connection – Connection - between The Being and the inhabitants of the Earth.

Towards the very end of the throng of Life manifesting in almost infinite mortal incarnations, he saw the birth of mankind. He saw their terrific rise after Earth's Millenia without their influence. He saw fantastic machines, wondrous inventions, uses of Earth, animals and fellow humans. Cultures were conceived, grew, flourished and passed, many into obscurity, forever forgotten. It was a great play, the greatest of all, being enacted before The Wanderers eyes.

He began looking for someone he knew; maybe a family member or friend that could be identified in this grand production. He was certain this was his home. However, while some of the characters seemed familiar, none were exactly the same as he could remember.

With the formation of the question in his mind, the vision faded and The Wanderer found himself again on the cliff overlooking the oasis. He looked at the Being.

"I saw things that looked like cars, but not quite. What were they? What was I seeing?" The Wanderer wanted to know everything about what he had seen.

"You were seeing the Earth; essentially the same one you live on now," The Being replied kindly.

"I was? Well, how come I didn't recognize those things? Some of those tools they used and other things I saw seemed… different. But the landscape itself looked familiar."

Believing he had seen an age as modern as his own – and probably his own – he continued, "Are my parents and my siblings and friends somewhere? Could I see them, too?"

There was a great, thunderous pause. "They do not exist."

"What? Why? How can my parents not exist? I don't understand," The Wanderer frowned.

"Please concentrate on what I am going to tell you," The Being slowly spoke. "To understand this, you will need to loosen your grasp on everything you think you know about the nature of reality. Everything must be a question for you at this moment to have a chance of comprehending on any level what you are about to see. You are in a dream state right now, in your mortal body. This is an advantage. So, what I say to you I also say to your dreaming Self who is observing our interaction: let go of what you think you know..." at this he gave a slight chuckle, "and watch."[9]

The Being again pointed towards the lake. As he obeyed, The Wanderer saw a reflection and was again enveloped in what he saw.

Encased in the deep blue, they saw a single light begin from its depths – similar to what he had seen before. The light grew to uncomfortable intensity and exploded.

---

[9] Any study of concepts relating to the nature of reality (ontology) require a flexible mind and an admission that what we think we know may not reflect the full reality. In fact, it could be argued that the more intensely we "know" something, the more we should consider it with suspicion.

This time as the light faded, instead of a Universe, The Wanderer saw something that could have been the center of it; a miniscule portion of the Creator and all of Creation at the same time.

This portion contained all knowledge and yet was only an experiment. It held the DNA to all answers, yet itself was only a question. As such, it was the ultimate riddle, the intersection between all opposites. There was a palpable feeling of love, happiness and play that emanated from this tiny portion of the Creator.

But it was wiser than that; this was no mindless thing. It was far gone in wisdom borne of all manner of pain as well, yet it laughed, not only in spite of all that it had encountered, but in joy because of it. As the shape of the center began to gain detail, to his horror and indescribable wonder he recognized this portion as himself, although far, far more by a spiritual recognition than a physical one. There was an innate beauty wrapped in the most delicious, humble sense of wonder and desire to explore than he could ever imagine. In his experience, the closest thing to this thirst to learn was something akin to that of a three-year-old child, but it had the life-experience of a very, very old man.

This could not be himself. Could it? There was no way. Still, there was a familiarity that he could not explain. He had to know.

"Is…is that me?" The Wanderer asked in a reverent whisper.

The Being smiled. "It is what is called your Intelligence. That means that what you see here is to be and is *simultaneously* clothed in all the physical manifestations the spirit will endure and enjoy. The reason what you are now seeing is not called a "spirit" is because your Intelligence is shapeless until it pre-informs each *physical* form the spirit will take. The formed essence of Intelligence, once manifested, is only then called a spirit."

The Wanderer looked back at The Being with a blank expression as the vision withdrew, and he found himself again gazing into His fathomless eyes.

Coming to himself more fully he said, "There are about three concepts there that make no sense to me. What did you mean when you said my Intelligence is simultaneously… what?"

"This is a distant concept for you because of your incorrect understanding of time as a linear dimension. I referenced it simply so we can come back to it later."

"OK, make that *four* concepts I don't understand..." The Wanderer said to himself in mock frustration (for he was immediately and completely comfortable with The Being as he would be any wise friend). "What do you mean that "time is a linear dimension?"

"It means that, like many things observed in nature, Time turns in a circle. Not coincidentally, Time looks like the number 8 in your language; a number of mortal power shaped like the conceptual symbol for infinity. Your culture views events like clothespins on a clothesline. It's not how it is."

"And it makes that much of a difference?" The Wanderer asked, eyebrows raised.

"Well, it makes no difference to Time, but it certainly makes a difference to any beings that concern themselves with it!" The Being said with a laugh.

"Why does it matter?" The Wanderer frowned.

"You are, to an extent, a product of the culture in which you have been immersed. This is why you currently see Time as a linear function; your culture has taught you that this is the case. But if any time-based culture is to survive, at some point in its existence the individuals in it must come to the point where such information becomes important to comprehend. If not mentally then certainly as a "felt sense"[i]."[10]

"What's a "felt sense"? The Wanderer frowned, shaking his head at the barrage of new terminology that was suddenly flooding his being.

"It's not easy to describe in your language, but it has to do with the state of mind that precedes identification with an object. It's the moment when the object is presented but before it is "named" by the mind. This moment can be very short for those that are habitually unconscious. In the end, ideas of this nature are not discoverable by the mind, only by conscious awareness," The Being patiently explained.

"You mean I have to be aware of the concept before I think I understand the idea behind it?" The Wanderer asked.

―――――――――――――――――――

[10] A "felt sense": getting the idea without placing words to it. In fact, the placing of words most often diminishes our ability to apply many concepts. This is the soulful science behind the koan, the true haiku, honest art and other practices including meditation. It is pure consciousness that flows into one's heart, before the mind gets hold of it to make it "useful", which the mind usually messes up due to flawed perspective. More in the Endnotes.

Time goes wandering
We lead it when we are lost
Peace found is timeless

—Tv

10/25/19

"No, it's more like allowing a sense of stillness to flow through you, dissolving the "you", so you become one with the truths that alight upon you."

Seeing The Wanderer's confusion, he added, "Don't worry. I'll help you see as we talk about these things. For now, just allow concepts you think you understand as rigid begin to soften. "Hear" more with your heart than worrying about the concept making sense to your mind, ok?"

The Being smiled with a sense of lightness that continued to put The Wanderer at ease.

The Wanderer nodded and The Being continued. "In any of Earth's incarnations where humanity is introduced, there are cultures that rise to dominance. If a culture is based on a view of Life that honors it, the culture thrives and all of life on the Earth benefits from it. If the culture is not based on this view, life suffers. There are a few conceptual caveats enjoyed by every healthy culture in eternity and space. A view of Time as non-linear is one of them. It allows an inherent wonder that is otherwise universally missing, at least from the members of a temporarily dominant culture."

"But why is it so important?" The Wanderer asked impatiently. "I still don't understand."

"It's important for two reasons. First, the act of naming is an act of judgement and betrays a serial attitude of separation: 'I am this, that is that.' Once named, any item is in danger of becoming categorized. Placed in a box, so to speak. Wonder is inherently dismissed, and the one who named it generally thinks they now "know," which disallows further teaching on the subject."

"I once heard that humility is the same as being teachable, and that pride is the opposite," The Wanderer offered. "You're saying that once we "know" something, unless we lose that feeling of knowing and come back to wonder, we can't learn more about the thing we named, right?"

"That's correct, and it applies to everything."

"Well, don't we have to name things? I mean, if I see an apple tree and want one in my yard, isn't it helpful to be able to tell someone I want an apple tree?"

"The problem isn't the naming," The Being explained. "It's the identification of the individual with the name. To use your example, if all you think you want is an apple tree, and you think you understand all an apple tree is, you've lost wonder and you're no longer teachable on the subject of apple trees."

The Wanderer nodded. "Oh, I see. It's not the naming then, it's the attitude that grows from the act of naming something?"

"Yes. The attitude doesn't have to accompany the name, but if a culture is tied to Time as a linear construct, then it follows that they will be identified with the naming of pretty much everything. The attitude simply follows the action. When a culture sees Time as non-linear, they're less likely to see a tree as linear. They're able to feel it's Being-ness more readily because the mind is less able to grasp the concept, leaving the heart to do so."

Nodding, The Wanderer said, "You mentioned two reasons that it's important for Time to be seen as non-linear. What's the second?"

"The second reason it's important is a little harder to explain, but it's because seeing Time in its proper relation to Life honors more accurately the concept of karma. It does this less dogmatically than you are used to, and more by way of a felt sense that we spoke about. It helps humanity initiate and eventually wholly integrate a kind of self-care that is critical for the survival of not only the culture and species, but of all of life. Again, this is true on any of Earth's incarnations."

The Wanderer considered this, his brow furrowed.

"Is this like saying, literally, what comes around goes around – since Time is shaped like an eight?"

The Being laughed. "That's pretty good, Wanderer! But, to answer your question, in a way it is, and in a way that's too simple. What a human does impacts all their spiritual incarnations at once."

"So, we experience a kind of simultaneous reincarnation? Is that what you're telling me? Our actions influence our spirits in the future and the past at the same time?"[ii]

"In a sense, yes. One spirit incarnation experiences different realities simultaneously. Each affects the other."

The Wanderer looked confused. "Well, if all my incarnations are simultaneously "clothed," and they are affected by each other, wouldn't the "later" ones be affected in such a way that they would consider their lives as pre-destined? I've never believed in that."

"A good enough question, but you're still trying to see this as a mental concept instead of feeling your way through the idea. That's ok, and it is enough for now on this topic except to say your incarnations feel what they feel, understand what they understand. Some of these understandings are based in truth or in various degrees of it. But when one makes a decided leap in consciousness or in understanding, all incarnations benefit. Pre-destination is a false concept that grew out of the very concept of linear time that we are discussing. But to further answer your question - and to potentially create a few more", he paused and smiled, "your spirits, which are literally without number, travel in "packs" of similar levels of understanding and consciousness – not together with *all* levels. Growth generally happens incrementally, not exponentially. Think of glacier travel, slow it down and multiply the slowing by eons and you'll begin to get the concept. But that's another conversation."

The Wanderer considered this and replied, "OK, so for now all I need to remember is that I have other parts or incarnations of me that affect each other in any given moment and that Time is not linear. I guess I can deal with that for now," he smiled. "It's a lot to take in, though. Why isn't there a religion that teaches this stuff?"

The Being chuckled and shook his head as he looked down at the lake, taking a deep breath. "It's a lot to take in with the mind, but as humanity awakens and begins to sense the value of Creation independent of it as an asset to be dominated, they are usually overwhelmed. All Beings belonging to the Earth inherently understand her Language at conception. It is the Language of the Creator, of Intelligence. It is familiar. It speaks of Home. But almost as a *condition* of mortality, particularly in less healthful cultures,[iii] humans get distracted from her. They hear her communications in fits and starts depending on their level of awareness at any given moment. A desire to communicate matters of consciousness or spirituality to others without the listeners having paid the price to gain the knowledge themselves…this is where religion most often arises."

"Wow," The Wanderer said, eyebrows raised, "that's another new concept to me; that religion is some kind of short cut! I always thought it was going about things the hard way. Can you give me an example of what you mean?"

"Sure, in general. A man that has forgotten the Earth's language finds himself without distractions in a place where the Language is spoken.[11] He feels and hears ideas in ways that seem familiar. It fills him with joy, wonder and a type of knowledge that allows wonder to coexist with it. These three things are always present when the Language is spoken. He feels these things not so much flowing into him, but as a feeling of recognition, as if he has always known the truth that is being communicated. He feels

---

[11] Solitude is one example.

expanded, enlightened, and in actuality he is. Then, he wishes to share his experience and his new paradigm. There are no spoken words to communicate what he has learned, or rather remembered, so he does the best he can. But in his exuberance, sometimes borne of a compassionate desire to share the fruit of his experience, he forgets that he had to learn in a certain way: no human could tell him these things, yet he wishes to teach."

The Being stopped and let what he said sink in before continuing. "Moreover, he may come to believe that he is a new vessel, called to tell the world what he has learned. But this is almost always counter-productive because except in very rare instances this is a thought tied to egoic wanting. Since he cannot begin to fully communicate what he was able to receive – let alone what he did not – he only gets part of the message to his audience. He may build a whole philosophy or dogma - or religion - around what he felt, but this serves ultimately to alienate his followers from their Source. This is because the people that hear and believe him now think they understand the topic *to the exclusion of others that they perceive as a threat to it*. They've named the apple tree, so to speak and are unable to learn more. Wonder, in other words, has departed.

Therefore, the followers cease to be true to the very essence of who they are; the tiny spark of light you saw at the center of yourself and all

Creation; their Intelligence, the essence of concentrated play and joyful seeking - and finding."[12]

"So, I could never share the things you're showing me?"

"Certainly, they can be spoken about, just like the apple tree might be. But it must be remembered that the concepts can't be fully described in any language of humans, although some languages are closer than others. Sanskrit, for instance, in the current incarnation of Earth is one of the closest, as are a few of the indigenous languages insofar as they are still pure – but at the moment with which you are most familiar now, most are dead or dying."

---

[12] In the book, "Siddartha" by Hermann Hesse, an ardent follower of the Buddha meets up as an old man and after many years apart with Siddartha, who had once been the follower's dear friend and fellow ascetic. His name is Govinda. In the discussion, Siddartha says to Govinda, "What should I possibly have to tell you, oh venerable one? Perhaps that you're searching far too much? That in all that searching, you don't find the time for finding?" Those that consider themselves "seekers" would do well to remember that finding should also be a part of their lives. Of course it is really all one and the same (the seeking and the finding), because if the finding doesn't bring more questions with it, it is probably a dead end or the "seeker" is becoming lazy or, worse, "knowledgeable".

The Wanderer frowned. "What's the point of having deeper knowledge if someone can't communicate it with anyone?" Then, answering his own question he added, "But I guess communicating it isn't the point as long as it is internalized by the recipient. A mute person can be inspired as well as any other, right? The point is to remember the Language."

The Being nodded in affirmation and added, "But man's ability to communicate spiritual truth is not really the core of your question. It is that mankind, once he thinks he understands a concept, immediately begins to wish to share it in the easiest way possible. This is both especially true and especially harmful when it concerns concepts related to consciousness and spiritualty. Since matters of this nature are not easily quantifiable, and since concepts can be communicated via the Language so quickly and thoroughly, the Teacher often ends up metaphorically teaching calculus to a third-grader. Add the Language barrier, and you have a situation where the teacher ends up describing, in essence, the pointing finger rather than that to which the finger is pointing.

The Wanderer nodded.

The Being continued, "To continue the example you requested, the man returns to his friends and instead of describing to them how he rid himself of distractions and meaningful communication came to him, he will describe what was communicated to him as some kind of universal truth."

"Well, isn't what was communicated to him, in actuality, Universal Truth?"

"Yes, what came to him was Universal Truth, but it cannot be adequately described or placed in its proper context because it was meant for him and him alone, for his benefit in that space and time according to the level of his preparation to receive it. Even if the message does apply to all of mankind it has to be individually felt to be communicated fully and internalized."[iv]

The Wanderer frowned. "I remember a teacher saying something about not giving someone "milk before meat." Is that what we're talking about?"

"That's very close. The point is that only the Giver of the Language knows where each individual sits in relationship to their mastery of more basic, "building block concepts" at that particular time, dimension and particular incarnation. Therefore, action must be taken by the listeners to duplicate the experience to attain real grasp of the concept. Words never suffice."

Do not teach me what you learned. Show me how you learned it.

The Wanderer paused and then said, "It sounds like the onus is more on the student than the teacher, particularly with concepts of consciousness. You can have a good teacher or a bad teacher, but if the teacher is the Giver of the Language, then the communication is perfect. So... again, it's up to the student to put himself in a place to hear the Speaker, which in that case would be the voice of Intelligence, the Language of the Earth. A teacher should also recognize the student needs this. Am I right?"

"Yes. Moreover, what the would-be mortal teacher might actually have heard might not have been truth in and of itself at all, since the Earth teaches by way of parable as well. The Earth also often allows the spirit of the Trickster[v] to teach. This aspect is an able teacher, too, but it is often labeled as something less than "good", if not wholly "evil".[13]

---

[13] Whether either exists without the other or if either exists at all is a question for the philosophers. Certainly we all have our preferences, but this is not the same thing. All too often we label that which we do not understand or wish to understand as "evil". Certainly there are aspects of "contrary energy" that seem to fly in the face of all of Life, but even these can have an effect that can be viewed as flowing with the energy of Life, or a final "positive outcome". However it takes more insight than we can usually muster to see this in the moment.

49

"Oh my gosh. Someone hearing the Voice of the Earth has to be careful of being fooled, too?"

"Well, trickery requires assumptions based on the one being tricked, right? Assumptions are a result of 'knowing', which comes as the result of the loss of curiosity and probably a rise of pride which, as the Biblical adage goes, "comes before a fall". Trickster energy is often used to show a human that they're identifying something with mind, to the exclusion of understanding with the heart."

The Wanderer sighed.

"The thing to remember is that to value any communication from the Creator is to sit in stillness with it and feel its message and the nature of it – whether a parable, something from Trickster energy or something to be taken literally. No religion teaches this because there is no value in it for the religion. And all religions – which always stem from the mind of mankind - are ultimately self-serving."

"No religion can have truth?" The Wanderer said skeptically.

"That's not what I said at all. They can, and they all do. That is the point. They all start with the intentions of a person or group of people to share a truth. Usually these intentions are honorable and honest. But because of the nature of the topic they end up not only falling short but fighting the very truth they were so enamored with in the first place because they can't fully describe it. The ideal "church" then, would be the most accessible of all: stillness in nature, free of both corporeal and mental distractions. With basic physical needs provided for – warmth, food, shelter – in time any man can hear the Language and get the experience for himself, which is as it was intended.

"I think I get it," The Wanderer smiled, wonder dawning in his eyes.

"Let's say the person that had the experience hearing the voice went back to her people and instead of communicating the message, she communicated the method for hearing it, having faith that each individual would receive what they needed in the way they needed it. Eventually, a felt sense of concepts that are conducive to Life would begin to guide more and more humans until they begin to make decisions that safeguard themselves, all of earth life and the Language of the Earth, which is really the Language of Intelligence, of Creator. When this occurs, eventually whole cultures simply begin to value the Voice more than the distraction from it. That's an amazing and beautiful thing to behold if they do it before the culture becomes seriously destructive."

The Wanderer smiled back. "There's certainly a lot to this... even more than I thought."

"To the mind, yes, it is a lot. But to bring it full-circle, your original question was quite simple. You asked, 'Is that me?' and I replied that it was your Intelligence. Before we move off this topic, let me add this; Intelligence is to Spirit is to mortal existence, what the subconscious is to thought is to action. And that is true for all the incarnations of individual Intelligences simultaneously."

The Wanderer sighed and looked down at the ground and gently shook his head, considering this. "I can live with that for now, I guess," he said.

"What I wish for you to hear at this moment is that at your core you are a part of All That Is, the ultimate Creator, and that your nature is to experience and learn, from the deepest depths of curiosity and play. You call yourself The Wanderer, and indeed you are. But while that name may have connotations of loneliness in your language, you will come to see that loneliness is not a concept that has any bearing in reality; only in an un-awakened mortal setting, and then only as a form of insanity."

"I still don't really understand, but I guess that corralling all this information into something that can be put into words, even to myself, is destructive to the message."

"I couldn't have said it better myself," The Being smiled, nodding.

"So, that's where this "felt sense" comes in? I need to feel the message under the words because that's where the truth lies, right? Because as soon as I try to put the "truth" into words, since language is limited, part of the truth is lost to me. Right?"

"Precisely." The Being smiled.

"I guess once someone starts to learn the Language of the Earth and begins to hear her messages to them specifically, if enough people hear this, the earth is saved, right?"

"It's not quite *that* easy," The Being said to The Wanderer as he turned his gaze back to the deep blue lake.

"I should just watch?" The Wanderer said with a wry smile, following the Being's eyes.

"You're beginning to get the idea..." he smiled back.

Enveloped again in the lake, The Wanderer saw something begin appear to come up from behind his formless Intelligence. It was an earth, growing larger and larger until it dwarfed it. As the earth had approached, The Wanderer's Intelligence itself had simultaneously changed in shape until it was the form of a tiny, beautiful hummingbird.

"Did the earth just come up behind my Intelligence? And am I now a hummingbird?" The Wanderer laughed.

The Being smiled. "The earth *appeared* to come up behind your Intelligence, but they are actually made of the same thing. More accurately, the world came into being *around* your Intelligence. And yes, your spirit form, and your soon-to-be mortal form, is in this case that of a hummingbird. It was – and is – your first foray into mortality."

The Wanderer turned and looked at The Being in wonder. "The Earth was created around my Intelligence?"

"You're beginning to comprehend, but remember what we were talking about before. Mental concepts such as that can actually be more destructive than constructive because your mortal nature is to identify an idea and make it absolute before it is complete, rather than to let the concept alight gently – like a hummingbird – allowing it to inform your Intelligence in *all* its complexity and simplicity. Failure to do this is how earnest, religious people can become inhuman monsters in the name of their gods, as happens from time to time throughout the histories of the worlds. Again, simply watch. And instead of merely taking in information with your mind, try to feel what is behind all of what you see."

As The Wanderer looked, his vision appeared to zoom in on an egg that was tucked into a tiny nest in a huge tree. The egg began to stir and was soon cracked from within. From it, he saw a tiny hummingbird emerge. He watched the parents of the bird feed it and keep it warm and safe from predators. In time, the tiny bird took flight. He saw it interact with other birds, eat food, drink water. He saw it mate and do everything a hummingbird would be expected to do. It lived a happy and relatively long life – before a snake caught and ate it.

The Wanderer laughed aloud, rejoicing in this play. He looked at the Being, who smiled back with the laughter of a child in his all-knowing eyes. The concept that he had lived more than one life was fascinating enough, but as a hummingbird as well? Was this why they had always been so special to him, especially as a child? [vi]

As he looked on, The Wanderer saw the snake live a while longer before it was crushed by a large stone that rolled off a mountain in a windstorm. From this point, he saw the same progression he had seen before; eons followed by humans. But this time, he observed something in the lives of the humans he had never seen before.

There was a great cultural war between those that had heard the Voice of the Earth and those that ignored it. The ones that heard it had spent their mortal time and effort learning the Language. Indeed, nothing else was ultimately of interest to them. Therefore, they did not live by all the rules that had been dictated by the culture and its spokespeople. They looked and acted at increasing odds with it and them. The powerful mortals on the other hand, while sensing at times a certain unknowable depth, had spent their time learning how to rule, govern, and make new products and systems that served the mortals in the short term, sometimes with devastating long-term physical and spiritual consequences.

When the ones that loved the Language rebelled against those that did not, the powerful ones attempted to quell their voices, which resulted in war and further insulation against the Language of the Creator. When the powerful ones later became tired of the insurrection, when it no longer served their needs, they used methods to control the others that were at such odds with the Life that the Earth itself retaliated – it actually defended itself - in myriad ways. Eventually the Earth won, ridding itself of the thing that was destroying it, preserving the physical Language of the Creator for another day.

The depth of sorrow that The Wanderer felt emanating from both the Earth and every being upon it was previously unfathomable to him. It was almost without end. It felt like the moment at the end of a child's scream when nothing is left to give, and yet the child continues to push air. The depth of death was inconceivable. There were no living things. Everything, from trees to mammals to birds to every creature of the sea, was dead. The vast amount of trash, crumbling buildings, bones, roads, vehicles, power plants, dams, and other detritus of a so-called progressive species lay rotting on an Earth that seemed less than lifeless. Nearly speechless, he turned to the Being, who returned his gaze calmly.

"It's almost too much to take," The Wanderer said in a whisper.

"Well, that's a good observation. It actually *is* too much for a mortal to take – which is why it is only shown in dreamtime, and then only to certain individuals, and then only in pieces."

"This is only a piece?" The Wanderer spoke to himself in wonder. Then, looking back at The Being he added "Is the Earth dead?"

"The Earth will never be entirely destroyed and it is older than mortals can ever comprehend. The carbon dating that some cultures use doesn't begin to touch her age because the assumptions made are incorrect.[14] But it is not entirely immortal; it will one day pass away into another form like all I have created. However, it will not allow itself to be destroyed until it is time. Moreover, because she is not only conscious but a highly-evolved consciousness, she will always defend herself when the time is ripe for her to do so. As a Being devoted almost solely to service, she does this for the sake of the others that need to hear her Language at any present or so-called "future time". It's important to know, too, that it is not mankind's nature to destroy the Earth any more than it is in an infant's nature to commit genocide. Both are acts of unconsciousness so extreme that they can only be termed as insanity. Mortals and cultures at this level of unconsciousness are so disconnected from the Language that they are eventually ruled solely by the desires of the moment and individual strength and will."

---

[14] Don't be impatient. You'll see why later.

"Well, it seems that everyone should see this! Maybe then we could do a better job of hearing the Voice through the Earth?

"That sounds a lot like a religion, Wanderer, doesn't it?"

"Well, if we know, we could prevent this!"

"Yes, but you've seen more here than you can ever explain, haven't you?"

"Yes," he admitted.

"Seeing this on a macro, final scale is not as helpful as a mortal human who is simply willing to see the pain they are causing themselves, one another and the Earth with enough compassion to awaken. They then begin to ask a very important question of themselves, whenever a new technology is introduced. The critical question is, "at what cost?" When culturally powerful, creative mortals ask this question in sincerity, the answer will come. They will be told where and who to ask and they will not be disappointed in the instruction."

"But from what I saw, the powerful ones had no interest in hearing what those that knew the Language had to say." The Wanderer frowned.

"You're right, in the incarnation that you saw, they did not."

"Then how will they ever make something different happen?"

"How do you think?"

"Well, the ones in power would have to care about the ones that know the Language or learn it themselves. Or care enough about the Earth herself."

The Being nodded. "And? What would happen then?"

"Well, I guess once they hear the Language themselves the ones in power would know what to do because the Voice, her voice – which is really the voice of Creator and even the voice of their own Intelligences - would tell them. They would know the right way to be. Not just for themselves, but for the ones they govern."

Nodding, The Being said, "Their actions begin to be infused with wisdom. And not only wisdom, but intelligence."[15]

"So, war...?" The Wanderer asked.

---

[15] ...or Intelligence, capitalized. Same thing.

"...ceases. Period." The Being spoke with finality.

"Pollution?"

"I think that's obvious?"

"Well," The Wanderer observed, "from what I've seen, the ones in power are so insulated from the Voice of the Earth that they will never hear it, let alone that of a puny human in their control that says they hear the planet talking to them. They would think they're the ones that are insane! Why would someone in power ever change, anyway? I mean, they're in power because they want to be in power, right? They choose power and insulation over a small voice in the wilderness. It's their decision."

The Being nodded. "You're right, it *is* their decision. They make the choice to be in power, even if they are born into it. A little aside here: what many people don't realize is that those born into what many call 'privilege' or 'power' are handicapped in a very clear way and deserve sincere compassion. They are, in effect, born into an insulated life. They are shielded from the Earth's Language almost from birth. Certainly, it is an easier life as far as physical comfort goes, but the cost – remember the question "at what cost" – is tremendous on a spiritual or consciousness level.

"I can't remember ever feeling sorry for someone born wealthy, but I get it," The Wanderer responded.

"Yes, it's a reality. But to get back to your question about people in power hearing the Voice, you're right. There is no impetus for them to change, to look at their actions, except one."

"What is that? What makes a person in power change to want to hear the Voice of the Earth when they have an easy, comfortable life?"

"Remember that rulers are still spiritual creatures at their center. They all look like you before you saw your essence changed into a hummingbird; full of light, play, curiosity. Early on, especially if they are born into privilege or power, they begin to insulate themselves from it, from the Voice of the Earth. They begin to see themselves as part of the culture primarily, rather than part of All That Is. They identify themselves through mental concepts that are incorrect, that are literally infinitely less. They hear the voice of personal egoic need, rather than the Voice of Life through the Language of the Earth. They begin very early and then very permanently to see no separation between their wants and themselves. This is at the heart of all war, all hatred, all heartache, even all apathy: the identification of the Self with the Object. And that identification is inherently inconsistent with anything that points to consciousness, which is the definition of eternity and Oneness."

"So how can that ever be changed?" The Wanderer held his hands and dropped them to his sides in exasperation.

"Pain," The Being spoke, almost reverently.

"Pain?" The Wanderer frowned. "Well, that doesn't make sense to me. I mean, they know they bring pain, don't they? Those in power always bring war, right? That's practically the *definition* of pain."

"They do and yes, they know and justify it. But I mean personal pain."

"OK..." The Wanderer frowned.

"You mentioned that if the culture is to awaken, those in power must also awaken. You've felt the truth of that statement. But those in power only awaken when they begin to see their current wants as separate from their deepest Selves. This takes a spiritual "crowbar", so to speak, because those two things, wants and the supposed "self", get fused pretty tightly. This crowbar has to have a physical or mortal aspect so it is handled by the Earth – the governing God of the physical realm. It also has a spiritual aspect because it is being applied for a purpose that is applicable to pure consciousness. For those in power to understand the difference between their eternal Selves and their wants in this space, the crowbar is used. Since those in power are focused on themselves above all others, the only Voice they hear is that of personal pain."

The Wanderer frowned. "So... they're *so* devoid of empathy that the only things that will motivate them to change the way they do things is if they feel something personal to them get taken away, beyond their control?"

The Being smiled, raising his eyebrows and nodding.

"I don't know about that. I've seen political leaders cry because of poverty, or war."

"Of course they cry, Wanderer. They feel pain, but until it's *personal* they are not motivated to go through the pain of change; of changing viewpoints, habits, procedures and policies. They know they face the pain of loss of status and that of humiliation by those that grant their power if they decide to change, if they lead that particular charge. If they feel the impetus at all, they're like children approaching the end of a diving board for the first time. They face the unknown and the uncontrollable, the wild and the wilderness of a soulful existence and fear it as they would death because of its unpredictability, because of its wild-ness. But this is the nature of Life. In short, they are afraid of Life. And many are simply unable to make the change."

"Well that's insane." The Wanderer shifted on his feet, looking toward the desert that had caused him so much anguish.

"Of course, it is!" The Being laughed. "You saw the destruction they allowed or caused."

"Well, is there any hope then?" The Wanderer looked like he was going to cry.

The Being paused and smiled softly, compassionately. "There is always hope. No matter what happens, there is hope.[16]"

---

[16] In fact, there is no need for hope on a spiritual level because of the Is-ness of Life. Hope springs from desire for an outcome. It is one thing to hope to be able to remember a passage from a favorite book. It is another to hope for "everything to work out" in some other life, or this one for that matter. This is not condoning apathy. Of course we should strive for what speaks to our deepest spiritual sensibilities, and many do: from tree-sitters to human rights activists to parents and religious leaders... and an occasional politician. Condoning a sense of contentment with "what is" in spite of or because of our worthy

○ Hope to accept
○ Hope to feel
○ Hope to know
○ Hope contentment

"Well, how? I mean, it seems like there would have to be enough pain felt by the powerful before they wage that final war on those they control. That culture I saw went from sick to critically ill very fast. That's probably a pretty small window of opportunity."

"You're speaking right now of any *one* incarnation,[17] which is an inherently flawed and mortal view, remember?"

The Wanderer nodded solemnly.

"But let's begin there with an example. Right now in the Northeastern part of the United States, a man in power resides. He is powerful in every visible way. He is handsome and in excellent health. He is in is late fifties, with graying hair, but his body is that of a man about two-thirds his age. He drives a car that costs far more than the median income of the people in the United States and his home is palatial, with the finest

---

efforts is the aim. That this can be difficult is an understatement. The Buddhist traditions seem to teach the practice of non-attachment more completely than others.

[17] At this point, most of The Wanderer's questions have to do with his current so-called incarnation. It is his only frame of reference. After all, he is a mortal, dreaming man. Therefore, he is taught from that paradigm until it expands. Which it will.

appointments and the most beautiful of art. He runs a company that is successful by every standard as well. It so happens that it supplies his government with materials that are used in defense. He receives awards, honor and praise for the defense of his homeland, even though he knows full well his products are used to go on the offensive as well. This man is divorced, and his ex-wife abhors him. He knows why but he doesn't think about it much because there is nothing that can be done, in his mind at least. This is generally indicative of his manner of coping with materials pertaining to consciousness – and mortal relationships of depth always do pertain to consciousness and karma. But the acceptance and perceived love of his sixteen year old daughter – her name is Maya - is the one thing this man covets more than his power, more than his status and more than his possessions, although he would seldom admit it even to himself. Of all he experiences on a day-to-day basis, her adoration is the one thing for which he would give it all up."

"Right now, she is taking a class in her private high school. Her teacher, Amy Mays, is one who consistently hears the Voice of the Earth and that knows the Language well. Amy has spent many weeks in solitude over the course of her life and has developed a love of stillness. She has developed ways to find it even in the midst of the temporarily dominant culture in which she necessarily and temporarily lives. She teaches Environmental Science, but she finds a way to work in some social and political science into her curriculum. She is about to assign a project that Maya will likely embrace that will change the course of her life. Maya will awaken as an environmental and political activist and her passion will get the interest of her father – especially when she refuses the gift of a very expensive sports car - simply because it is not fuel efficient."

"He will try to shrug it off as youthful exuberance but her act of defiance will sit with him and will prepare him to hear facts that she subsequently relays to him in her enthusiasm over the following weeks. These will all work themselves into his subconscious. He will be disturbed, bothered, because he has been trained by Maya herself to pay attention to her when she speaks. This strong young woman insists on that kind of attention from him for her to return his adoration."

"The facts themselves that he hears will be compelling. He will feel a measure of cognitive and spiritual dissonance that has been unknown to him for many years. It will be a very real dissatisfaction on a level that he did not even feel when he passed through his difficult divorce. At first, he will not know how to deal with it. This is where many who wish to remain unaware and fearful may attempt to cover their pain with further distraction – alcohol, sex, drugs, spending, and murder[18]

---

[18] I hate to say it, but another addiction/ distraction appears to be the

among other things. But if he indeed goes into the pain to see what it is about, the result will be that he will take some time to arrange his affairs and then completely shutter the company."

"He will cease his service to the destruction of the Language of the Earth. And his life," here The Being chuckled again and shook his head in wonder, "will be immeasurably richer for it. As will his daughters'."

The Wanderer considered all this. "How will we know if he takes the path of going into his pain? What's that look like?"

"He will have many paths that he can take, including, as I mentioned, the path of further distraction. But looking at him now, I feel his spirit is ready to take another. The project that Amy is about to assign Maya's class will culminate in a three-day excursion to some islands off the coast of the eastern United States, in Chesapeake Bay. Here they will study soft shell crabs to document the effects of the very chemicals that Maya's

---

"news" (often nothing more than propaganda) or any information source that continually and consistently reinforces our already-held beliefs, making us ever more "right" and the others increasingly "wrong". The wisest people I know make it a habit to revisit all sides of an argument from time to time. This can either strengthen current beliefs or give needed insight and, ultimately, compassion – one of the highest of all human traits.

father's company has discharged for years into the rivers that feed the Bay. As always, Amy will introduce a subtle spirituality to the excursion that will include meditation and other stillness practices before and after the days' work."

"At her request, Maya's father will attend with her as a chaperone. He will see the event with some cynicism at first but, as I mentioned, he will likely be swayed by Amy's enthusiasm and the depth of her soul along with Maya's enthusiasm, illustrated initially by the act of the refusal of his expensive gift. As he deepens his interest in his daughter's passion, he will be visited by the spirits of the beings his company affects: the soft-shell crabs, sea birds and fish of the Bay. They will come to him in thoughts during the day and also in the dreams of the night. If necessary and if they feel he will be receptive, the indigenous peoples that were displaced generations before have power to visit him as well, also usually in dreams, but sometimes making their presence felt in odd occurrences and seeming coincidences. Instead of going into distraction, I believe in this incarnation he is ready to remember the Voice of the Earth." With a smile he added, "I'm usually not wrong."

"OK, that's *one* guy…" The Wanderer said, raising his eyebrows and shaking his head.

The Being's face fell and he looked at him sternly. "That's how it always is, and that is always the response of the unaware, Wanderer. Just as it takes millions of snowflakes to make an avalanche, cultural shifts and revolutions always start with the first human. Always. Your response completely dismisses the force of momentum, the idea that one plus one can, in effect, equal three." He paused then added, "And it also illustrates the belief of the one making the comment that that they actually know what's going on in their plane, and that they actually know how things work, hmm?"

The Wanderer looked sincerely chastened as he said, "I'm sorry...can you show me how it works? How is it effective for this one man, as powerful as he is, to make a change?"

"Well, I want you to understand that it didn't start with this man. It didn't even start in his family. It started three generations ago in Amy Mays' family when her great grandfather decided to make the sacrifice to save the family farm in upstate New York, rather than sell it and move to Albany during a few particularly difficult years. Asahel Mays is his name. It was the property that he preserved that Amy's grandfather, father and then Amy herself used to learn the Language. The Language taught and requires, as it always does, a type of stillness that inhabits those that know and can remember it in spite of distractions. The Earth becomes their

temple and oracle; not necessarily something to worship –
although there is certainly no harm in this since it is, as I said,
the governing God of the physical realm. But more importantly
it is something to worship *within*. Amy spent as much time as
she possibly could with her father, also a small farmer. So, you
might say that the first snowflakes in Maya's father's personal
avalanche started generations ago. It will continue in this way,
with a young political activist named Maya, and then with
himself. Many people will lose jobs when he closes his business,
but because his core is still compassionate it is still in his nature
to be more than generous to those that are so affected so their
suffering is minimized. These people will know the reason;
indeed, the whole eastern seaboard will be aflame with talk of
the powerful business owner that shuttered his company after
"the Environmentalists got to him." The threats he will receive
from the government that once awarded him will only galvanize
his resolve. Most of his competitors will be happy for the
sudden void in supply and will rush to fill it, but the fact that the
well-respected businessman left will be the first inkling of
awakening for a few more powerful people. Several will reach
out to him personally, by phone, in a restaurant or golf course
and really ask him about his choice. Some may be similarly
affected."

"One of them will likely be a man in Chicago that owns a
company that supplies Maya's father's company. He is made of

different stuff: he is happily married and has been faithful to one woman with several well-adjusted children. He will call Maya's father on the phone and they will have a series of communications that will affect the way that the man from Chicago does business as well. He employs seven hundred people. Most will note the change in the way the business operates and understand why; to preserve the earth, at least according to the owners' new-ish beliefs. Some will be personally moved to do more themselves in their smaller spheres of influence. Without going into more detail, the effect of the closing of Maya's father's business will spread to powerful men and women in San Francisco and Seattle, and from there to Japan. So, you can see... it's fruitless to say, ever, "it's only one guy." It's *always* only one guy, alone with his pain, or fear of pain. And pain is the ultimate crowbar to separate what remains from what is temporary."

"Well, wait a second," The Wanderer interjected. "It seems like this guy might be motivated by love, not pain."

"Yes, it does seem that way. But as "good" a man as he is by some standards, he is still consistently unaware of anything greater than himself. Inasmuch and to the extent that as this is the case, his love always has a component of fear. In this case, it is the fear of loss, specifically the loss of the love of his daughter. It is this pain he wishes to avoid."

"Hmm..." The Wanderer mused.

"Now, his motivation is not *only* that. He has a natural curiosity, a level of self-honesty and inquiry, standards of behavior and enough of an ethical base to serve him, even when his understanding expands and he begins to hear the Voice. He is not always unaware. It is important to note that he is simply *consistently* unaware.[19] This is true of the vast majority of the players in the culture in which he resides. They are generally sleepwalking, with moments of inspiration. These moments take hold when the mortal is ready."

An aside: the way The Being was talking to The Wanderer...this was really something to behold. The words sounded at times like chastisement, but there was a feeling of lightness and laughter underneath it that is indescribable. The topic was serious; there is no doubt The Being was not joking with The Wanderer, but it was a message that traveled on pure love, on the holiest concern for his audience. That, as much as anything, has helped me communicate more effectively since The Dream. It can't be faked, the type of love that The Being demonstrated, but it *can* be imitated until it can flower. That's what I've done

---

[19] He's not dead, he's only *mostly* dead. Sorry, "The Princess Bride." You understand.

as I've tried to go into stillness and to learn the Language, and it is slowly working (as fast as I allow).

But what about remembering what it is that we've learned?

Many of us find ourselves caught in the trap of making the same mistakes over and over. Some of us pay for expensive spiritual retreats and are not disappointed; we truly come back inspired, with new tools to help us in our quest to meet higher expectations of ourselves. But anyone who has made these investments knows well that the feeling and newfound inspiration last only so long before they find themselves in the same ruts as before. There may be a little different flavor to them (or not), but they are familiar at the very least. So how can we remember what we've learned? The Wanderer asked the same thing.

"You've mentioned distractions, and how this is the main problem with the temporarily dominant culture. When the culture was rising, I saw the number of things that people had to distract themselves grew as well. You mentioned the people born into wealth and privilege, how insulated they are, so they forget early in life and have to re-learn the Language. The more powerful the people, the more things they have to distract themselves, and the more they want. Getting more and more distractions into someone's life gets to be an addiction, from what I saw," The Wanderer commented.

"Yes, that's true in almost every incarnation. What is your question?"

The Wanderer added in a thoughtful voice, "Even things like food – something someone needs to live – gets to be a distraction. Music, sex, like you mentioned before... I even saw some people who call themselves "spiritual seekers" distracted from the Language of the Earth by their so-called seeking. And those that the powerful ones ruled...sometimes they were as distracted as the powerful, just in a different way. Towards the end of the earth incarnation that I saw, hardly anyone experienced real stillness."

"Those are all correct observations," The Being replied. "I still don't hear a question."

"Well, does it always have to come down to pain? Is that the only... crowbar? How can a person that is addicted to distraction ever hope to learn the Language of the Earth, let alone implement it?"

"Keep going," The Being encouraged. "Explore what it is that makes the question arise."

Continuing, The Wanderer said thoughtfully, "It seems like those that value the Language can see their need to get away from distractions, and many do just that. And when they're away and they feel the Language of the Earth - they feel the words of the animals and rocks and clouds and trees, and they cry because it's so beautiful and they vow to not forget. And then they get back into the culture and within a few weeks they're right back in the thick of it, like they never left. So, I guess my question is, exactly how toxic and addictive are distractions? Is it possible to ever really break free from them, or is it that the moment they appear and work themselves into everyday life, that the person is doomed to suffer pain?"

"Good question, but you've seen part of the answer, haven't you?"

The Wanderer nodded. "I'm curious about Amy. She seems to have figured out ways to live without distraction. Well, less distracted, anyway."

"There are many others as well, but yes, Amy Mays will work well in this example. Look into the lake again. I think that will illustrate an answer to your question."

Standing on the cliff, The Wanderer and The Being looked into the now familiar glasslike water and were swallowed by the great blue.

They saw a little dark-haired girl about nine years old running full-speed out of a small farm home holding a paper bag. The screen door slammed against the house as her mother yelled something after her. Dust leapt up from the tired earth under canvas shoes of the same color. She wore jeans and a t-shirt. It appeared to be late summer. Everything the girl passed was green, lush. The earth was showing its abundance in the fruit that hung from vines and trees; grapes, blackberries, blueberries, plums and apples. But the little girl, running as fast as she could with grey explosions of dust behind her, was not interested for now.

"Is that Amy?" The Wanderer whispered.

"That's her, as a little girl in this incarnation," The Being whispered back, reverently.

As The Being and The Wanderer watched, the little girl ran up behind a green tractor making its way to a field at the end of a long dirt road. "Daddy! Daddy! I have lunch for us!"

A ruddy, bearded man with kind eyes stopped the tractor and, with a huge hand at the end of a proportionate arm, hoisted the little girl and her package up onto the tractor and sat her on the fender next to him. They sat under a canopy of oak trees, eating sandwiches commensurate with their respective sizes. There was no music to turn off, no headphones, no motor. There was nothing besides the natural world around them.

They talked about Amy's day so far and where her father was going on the tractor and why, further building her already impressive knowledge of seasons and the earth's rhythms. Then they ate in silence for a few minutes before Amy spoke again.

"Daddy," Amy asked, "you know how Amber moved into the city?"

"Yes," her father replied, looking into her eyes thoughtfully.

The little girl swallowed and looked at the ground. "She says they're going to be rich now because her dad got a job there. I'm going to miss her."

"Yes, it's hard when friends move away, isn't it?"

"Why do we stay out here then? Why don't we move into the city, too?"

"Well, your mother and I have thought about that, sweetie. We used to talk about that quite a bit. You know, I went to college. I graduated with honors."

"What's that mean?"

"It means I did well there. My professors thought I was pretty smart. I could get a good job in the city somewhere. But there are tradeoffs your mother and I chose not to make."

"Tradeoffs? Like what?" the little girl asked, frowning.

"Well, for instance, if I worked in the city, I couldn't sit outside on a beautiful summer day with my favorite girl in the world, eating lunch on my tractor. I would have to be in an office, eating lunch while I worked, probably. I would have to drive a couple hours each day – and that whole time I would be far away from you and your mom and brother. It would be an easier life in some ways, but harder in all the wrong ways for our family. It would have been too high of a cost for us. Does that make sense?"

Amy frowned. "What do you mean by high cost?"

"Well, I mean that sure, it would be nice to have a newer truck or car and believe me, there are times in March when it's raining sideways and I am cold and wet to the skin and it's only noon…," he chuckled, "sometimes an easier life sounds pretty good. But trading in all the good times, like this one, because of a few bad ones seems like a bad trade for our family to your mother and me. It would come at too high a cost. Does that make sense?"

"You mean you wouldn't trade lunch with me for anything?" The smile was sincere and priceless.

Amy's father's eyes laughed as he smiled. "You got it, cutie." And then he added in a serious tone, "Always remember, Amy, to ask what things cost. It's not always in dollars. Sometimes the cost is measured in how good or bad life will be after you get what you think you want. It's like eating cherries. You think you want to eat a whole tree full of them when they first come out, don't you?"

Amy nodded, her mouth full.

"Well, what would be the 'cost' of eating all those cherries?"

Amy smiled and laughed. "Diarrhea!"

Her father chuckled with her and tousled her hair. "And we wouldn't know anything about that, now would we? So, the cost of too many cherries is a sick tummy, right? So it makes sense to eat a few so you can really, really enjoy them. Your mother and I used the same idea to make a decision about how to live. Some money is good, but wanting too much can make you make choices that make you sick. We feel like we have enough. It seems like it would be nice to have more sometimes, but… let me ask you, Amy, what do you think the costs of me working in the city would be?"

"Well, I don't know…I guess you would have to get a new job?"

"Yes, and if I got a new job, what would that mean for the family?"

"Well, we would have more money. But we also might have to move, and you would be at the office all the time, and we wouldn't be able to have lunches anymore."

"Yes, and I would have to drive more which is not good for the earth, and I would miss being outside, and seeing your mom during the day, too. These aren't big tradeoffs by themselves – lots of people make them – but they all add up, like lots of little cherries. Too many changes, like too many cherries, might make our whole family sick."

Amy thought about this a few moments. "Is Amber's family going to get sick?"

Amy's father smiled at her kindly. "I don't know what will happen to Amber's family. It's hard to say what is best for someone else. I can barely find out what's right for me, let alone other people. Their circumstances may be totally different than ours, so this may be the best thing for them. All you can do is keep being Amber's friend. They'll probably be just fine."

"But she won't be able to have lunch with her daddy, like I get to!"

The big man shook his head. "No, she probably won't."

The Wanderer saw this and many more conversations like it, sometimes on a tractor, sometimes while cleaning out a chicken coop, sometimes while canning peaches that Amy had picked.

Very seldom was there a radio playing. Smart phones were out of the question. They did not even appear to own a TV.

The Wanderer saw that in the background of Amy's life, there was silence. But it was more than that: there was a budding connection to stillness that she took with her into many interactions. The Wanderer saw this connection called many things by those who observed her; "mature for her age", "an old soul" and, sometimes, "too serious".

In fact, Amy was not particularly any of those things. She was completely normal physically and physiologically, apart from the stillness that seemed to have chosen her.[20]

The Wanderer and The Being watched her grow into young adulthood, making choices that sometimes took her away from stillness and sometimes toward it. However, since she had had a taste of it early in her life, it was to that state she returned when she felt that her life was not what she wanted.

There was a time early in her teenaged years, for instance, when she had come home from school particularly discouraged. Instead of talking to her mother or father about her concerns,

---

[20] Stillness sometimes *appears* to choose those that possess it, as if the Universe favors them. Ultimately this is ludicrous. While there may be some physiological differences that predispose one to be able to access stillness easier and more readily than another, unless there are reasons greater than I have space to get into here, generally speaking any healthy mortal is able to do so.

she went to a particular tree in an overgrown orchard not far from her house, climbed up and munched on a late pear from the branches. Sitting in silence, and then stillness, she felt the cares lift from her. It was, for all intents and purposes, her first practical attempt at meditation. Thirty minutes later the issue remained, but attachment to an outcome was missing. She found, in spite of her situational preference, that she had a resource, a friend, a kind connection that would remain with her no matter the outcome. Hence, all would be acceptable in the end.

With this Stillness as a partner, she became an increasingly able student with all the necessary tools at her disposal to identify, pursue and attain her dreams that were in accordance with it.

From this and other experiences she began to sense even more deeply the difference between silence, Stillness and strife and to see where Stillness could be reliably found.

Later, The Wanderer and The Being smiled as they watched her learn how to take Stillness with her instead of having to retreat from distraction to find it, a beam of light through an otherwise impenetrable fog.

Seeing this, The Wanderer looked at The Being and shook his head in disbelief. He felt filled with light, unable to tell the smallest part of what he felt.

"Wow," was all he could say, his voice filled with wonder as he chuckled.

Chapter Six: Life Practice

The Being smiled. "What strikes you about Amy?"

"Well," The Wanderer said thoughtfully, "Two things, I guess. It's as if... it's as if, when she was growing up, she didn't have to go back through layers of noise to find silence, and she was surrounded by living things that spoke the Language of the Earth. I mean, they had chickens, pigeons, ducks, dogs, cats and geese. They had peaches, pears, apples, raspberries, blueberries and figs on their farm. It didn't look very big, though. Was it?"

"No, it wasn't. Her father, Johnson Mays, did most of his farming on land nearby that was controlled by others. But what did you get from what you saw?" The Being smiled, "That the secret to deep hearing and not forgetting the Language of the Earth is to have quiet and chickens?"[21]

"There's more to it than that?" The Wanderer deadpanned. "No, I think it helps that she was surrounded by things that were alive but that manifested a different kind of Life than hers. She could see that a duck or a hydrangea had Life, just like she

---

[21] I know some fine people in Portland, Oregon who seem to believe this.

did. It's just that the way that Life manifested itself physically was different from the way it manifested in her. The only difference was in the physical realm, nowhere else. This taught her real empathy and deep respect for all living things, I think. But on the other hand, it's almost as if she sensed that care for the life around her was more than simple empathy; it was more like self-care, right?"

The Being raised his eyebrows and nodded. "OK, how so?"

"Well, as I mentioned, I think she sensed that she was more than similar to the Life she saw around her. I think she, on some level, felt a part of it, and that it was a part of her on a level that she didn't understand with her mind, or need to, or care to."

"Those are good insights." The Being said approvingly.

"I know I already said this, but the fact that Amy's parents arranged their home in such a way that she could find a place of silence pretty easily, and because silence was present, stillness was accessible. Because there wasn't so much noise, there could be less distraction. After all, she was just a student of stillness at first, right?" The Wanderer asked.

"Yes, but I think it's important to point out that they did not live a monkish existence, either."

The Wanderer shook his head in agreement. "No, of course not. It looked like a pretty close community, from what I could see. There were often visitors, work parties... The Mays' worked hard - and a lot - but there was plenty of playtime and entertainment among themselves and the community as well. It's just that the overriding condition was that of silence... well, maybe it was more like there was just no unnecessary noise. It wasn't quiet, necessarily. But silence was valued so noise, which..." here The Wanderer paused, considering concepts that seemed to be streaming into his mind, "...seems to come from things that distract people... was just diminished." Pausing again, he added, "I guess the things that distract members – or prisoners – of many cultures generally produce a lot of noise. Does that make sense?"

"Sufficiently, yes. But there is a slightly deeper difference between silence and stillness that you haven't mentioned. Can you think of what that might be?" The Being spoke like the kindest, gentlest school instructor there could ever be.

The Wanderer paused again, seemingly tapping into something within himself that he had once almost forgotten was there. "Well, silence is absence, the absence of noise, right? Kind of like black is the absence of color. Stillness, instead, seems to be the presence of something deep, an "inner knowing" grounded in a connection to our... well, I think it's being grounded through our spirit all the way back to our Intelligence?"

The Wanderer now paused, considering a concept that would have been absolutely incomprehensible to him a day ago. It now seemed like something he'd known and understood for eons and was simply remembering. Continuing and nodding, he said, "Yes, that seems right. But when she was learning to sense stillness, she needed times of silence like anyone would. Otherwise she would be too distracted to ever learn it. And Stillness is the only place where the Language can be heard."

The Wanderer paused, considering his own words and processing them almost as if someone else had spoken them.

The Being watched him with approval, and after a moment added, "You essentially said that silence is to Stillness what black is to color. Did I state that accurately?"

The Wanderer nodded, considering this. "Yeah, I think so."

"A human, then, that senses stillness is actually in possession of an asset, and this asset is an informing one. It's not absence, but Presence. If Concepts themselves are Teachers, then Stillness is the ultimate Schoolmaster, the gatekeeper to all Concepts and innate Wisdom."

"Unbelievable," The Wanderer said in response. "I had no idea that Stillness was so... well, it's almost corporeal, isn't it?"

"Yes, just as Time is more corporeal than non-corporeal in nature, so is Stillness."

There was a long silence as these concepts seemed to sink into The Wanderers consciousness.

"So back to Amy's story," The Wanderer continued, "it was important for her to find physical, emotional and mental places of non-distraction when she was young. That way, she could not only hear it, but learn to value it. Having parents that felt and lived this way helped her as well; it was critical to her ability to teach, later in life."

"Very good. But you saw how she moved through the world in her later years, right?" The Being asked The Wanderer. "This is not a woman that sat at home on a meditation cushion all day."

"No, it was amazing how she learned how to take stillness with her. I think her parents were like that, too." The Wanderer paused. "It seems like she was pretty lucky to have had parents like this, but I get the feeling that it's not required to have that kind of upbringing to hear the Language. That doesn't seem consistent with Creation – it would seem too … privileged… like a person born into royalty or something. The Universe doesn't act like that."

"Well," The Being challenged, "genetic characteristics of parents are passed down in any instance to children. Maybe she was more predisposed to finding stillness?"

"I see your point, but we kind of already spoke about this. It seems that human mortality is ultimately a quest for a consistent spiritual connection in a physical plane, so it has to do also with the strength of the will of the spirit. It can't wholly be a question of physical ability or genetics, right? Sure, it seems within the bounds of the justice of the Creator to allow one a… a *talent*, I guess… for one finding stillness over another. Amy's "talent," so to speak, handed down from her parents, was the gift of a true home. A refuge. Physiologically, maybe they were also not given to flightiness, or such busy minds. Maybe they were simply the type of people that could sit still, enjoying both the emptiness of silence and the presence of stillness. But I think that has to be the extent of it. She still had to make the choice to embrace the gifts, spiritual and physical, that her parents gave her. Am I right?"

"For most of what you said, yes, you are correct. One point you make was based on the assumption that all Spirit is on earth in a physical form to come to awareness, to stillness. That is not *always* the case,[22] but this is an assumption that has to be made in every case by every sentient being: that they are here to come to deep awareness through stillness, whether that is the case or not."

"Ok, I'm not going to ask about that," The Wanderer held up his hands and closed his eyes for a moment in mock defense. "That seems like a can of worms. All I need to remember right now is that it's not required to have parents that know anything about stillness for an individual to find it in and for themselves."

The Being nodded in agreement. "Of course. By the way, the concept I did not share is not too difficult but it's not entirely necessary right now." Then he added, smiling. "We can spare you, this time."

---

[22] Some individuals are here fulfilling a commitment made in a separate plane. To these, stillness may not be a part of that commitment – indeed, real stillness may prevent them from bringing to bear the personality that is needed for another's trial or blessing. For our purposes, it is important that this concept is not used as some kind of excuse not to be interested in accessing stillness in this plane. Even a person that has some kind of karmic music to play that is hard to hear may have as a part of his gifts the process of awakening and positively influencing those around him, no matter the bugbear he had once been.

The Wanderer chuckled. "Thanks."

"But regarding what you said about inheriting some kind of advantage at birth that somehow makes finding stillness easier for some over others in the throes of a temporarily dominant culture like Amy's, you're right. If having aware parents were a prerequisite to stillness, not too many people in the last years of these cultures would have a chance because most parents are themselves nowhere near stillness, either. People in those times that are trying to find stillness have to find a thread of reason for doing so. They must see the inherent insanity or suffer some kind of personal pain – like we discussed – or recognize someone that can show them a reason for making the effort to stop identification with the shifting sands of their own egos. It's about seeing they've been distracted. Distraction being, of course, the hallmark of all latter power-centric cultures."

"I understand, but I have a couple questions. The first has to do with a term you used: "latter power-centric cultures." The second is, 'what tools do people have that aren't like Amy, that don't have teachers nearby?'"

The Being frowned. "What do you mean, 'don't have teachers nearby'? Of course, teachers are everywhere."

"They are? What if someone doesn't know anything about stillness? What if they don't know about the Language? How would they know to look for a teacher of these concepts?"

"Does the presence of a potential Teacher mean there is a student that is willing to learn? Of course not. Moreover, we've already established that personal pain itself is an able Teacher. Exquisite pain can make any person pause in most instances. But it's not the only Teacher."[23]

"Well, what are some others?"

"Do you remember the case of Maya's father? He isn't looking to be awakened. What are some potential Teachers for him?" The Being countered.

"OK, Amy Mays was going to be one, and his daughter. The way he felt about his daughter is a good one!"

"Yes, good. That's correct, even though that love is technically impure because it also contains fear, which is an opposite of

---

[23] ..unless it doesn't. We've all known people that have become embittered rather than humbled by their challenges and pain. That seems to be the choice; approach stillness humbly as one would the mythical "man on the mountain" or internalize it as some kind of divine vendetta and watch the soul harden to life, Life, love and Love.

love. He's afraid of losing his daughter's adoration, so imperfection in his love is implied. But the Teachers that surround all humankind know this and are ordained to reach into that imperfection when the time is right. You've heard the saying, 'when the student is ready, the teacher will appear'? This is accurate. And perfect love, or perfect motivation of any kind, is not required. Although the purer the motivation, the more able the student will be to withstand the schooling."

"Ok I get that. And you also mentioned the spirits of the animals and even some people would maybe visit this man in his dreams."

The Being nodded, adding, "And in seeming coincidences, which are, of course, a fallacy."

"OK, so the powerful man in the East, Maya's dad, he begins to become aware of the Language of the Earth, right? But he has a long way to go from where he is. Do the Teachers...well, I guess they know what and how much to give him? And then it's up to him to be taught?"

"Correct on both accounts. If he doesn't distract himself from the pain of potential rejection from his daughter, one or many Teachers will be with Maya's father every step of the way. Sometimes he will listen and be taught, other times he may not.

Because his love is imperfect, his walk on this new path will likely be imperfect. But that's okay; once the conceptual schooling has begun, how "sleepy" he is, or, after how willing he is to release or "forget" the helpful concepts he's learned on the path, will determine the amount of pain he will experience along the way. How much he esteems his learning in spite of pain is how it's determined how much he values it, by the Concepts themselves."[24]

"I'm beginning to see how important it is to be taught by the Concepts themselves," The Wanderer said.

"Yes, it's critical. And, if and when he makes decisions away from the lessons he's acknowledged once he's started down the path, personal pain is always waiting to jab him, to wake him again and to help him hear. Among pre-mortal human spirits it is well known and accepted that within a mortal sojourn they will be surrounded by pain. They all know what they are getting into. It has a specific purpose and it is unique to the mortal experience."

"Is it always about pain?" The Wanderer thought about his time in the desert, a seeming eternity ago.

---

[24] "Our destiny is to live out what we think, because unless we live what we know, we do not even know it." Thomas Merton, Christian mystic 1915-1968.

"Oh, of course not. It's most often the first Teacher, but there are many other compassionate Teachers as well. For instance, as self-compassion grows he will allow himself to acknowledge personal growth within himself. Gifts of patience and the increased ability to enjoy his life will become more frequent. And he may feel the stirrings of other gifts that he has habitually covered his whole life through distraction. This man, for instance, has a gift as a healer that has been cultivated over many lifetimes. He may or may not get to develop it fully – his time in this incarnation does have its limits – but to the extent he does develop it, it will be a tremendous gift for him and others as he becomes increasingly familiar with The Language."

"Wow. Wow!" The Wanderer, shook his head in amazement. "So much going on around this guy! And it's like this for everyone?"

"Yes, of course. All Intelligences, as a part of All That Is, are willing and able to experience spirit-hood and mortality specifically because they know that personal pain will provide the parameters that will allow them to stay on course, on mission. Of course, that may or may not be effective, it's up to each, but that is a known "risk" as well, so to speak. It is, at any rate, to be expected and is part of the experience of All That Is experiencing Itself. In the end there is no real way to get it wrong since the final judgment remains only in the will to act, to experience. The second matter, how "asleep" one remains in mortality, is merely a function of the amount of pain those "clothed Intelligences" are willing to endure, or how much they are obliged to allow distraction to cloud their vision. What they actually learn while so clothed is not the primary concern. The point is the experience. But there is, as you can see, an effect to their actions on themselves and their fellow travelers, human and non-human."

The Wanderer paused, letting the words sink into him. He had questions flooding his mind, but he knew that to ask further on this subject would be ultimately fruitless - that his mind would latch onto the words, somehow ruining his understanding of the concept.

Sensing the presence, approval and stillness of The Being himself washing over him, he made the conscious choice to proceed, hoping to try this stillness another time alone to see if this could somehow plumb the depths of this idea from that platform.

He took a deep breath - it was more like a sigh - and asked, "OK. Can you tell me what you meant by 'latter power-centric cultures'? You said that a while back."

The Being, his eyes alight with something that seemed like honor being bestowed upon his pupil replied, "I meant to refer to temporarily dominant cultures in their early death throes; the 'latter' end of their temporary dominance."

"You're making a point to say 'temporary'. Why? It seems redundant," The Wanderer frowned.

"Because it's more accurate, there are words for it, and to remind you that any culture that disregards, let alone fights against, its own environment and its own spiritual nature is, by obvious definition, temporary. Aside from its failure to ask the question 'at what cost', the mistake that the participants in temporarily dominant cultures make is to forget the impermanence of their day-to-day experience, making attachment to it fruitless. Impermanence is, of course, the one constant of mortal life. It defines Life – something you pointed out earlier when we were talking about people in power and how they fear Life for its "wildness". A fundamental understanding of the concept of "Soul as Wild" is an acceptance of the impermanence of Life. This acceptance is critical to awakening a culture. And this deep understanding takes it from fighting against itself and Life, precluding as it does not only war but all anger; anger being another hallmark of temporarily dominant cultures."

"*All* anger is?" The Wanderer raised his eyebrows.

"Yes, all anger," The Being replied. "Anger is never in accordance with Intelligence. It is always the marriage of fear and ego."

The Wanderer considered this, still skeptical. "Well, what if someone is being attacked and needs protecting?"

The Being raised his eyebrows. "Is anger really necessary in this case? No, anger actually *requires* a disassociation from Intelligence to manifest in mortality. By the way, of course the helpless should be physically protected. This act can be one of great awareness, but anger need not be a part of it. Intelligence is never angry; Intelligence simply *is*, just like the Creator from which Intelligence springs. Anger is generally caused by frustration which is caused by an attachment by a mortal to an outcome that is not being satisfied in a mortal plane to the ego's preference.[25] The mortal who is attached to a specific outcome in danger of not being realized, is frustrated and fearful. He may see in the moment no alternative but anger, accompanied by force, if possible. Since Intelligence dwells in a

---

[25] Specifically, the mortal plane in which the angry mortal resides. The angry mortal disregards all other potential realities and at least temporarily eschews any greater purpose for the situation in which he finds himself.

state of Presence that has a deep knowledge of the impermanence of spiritual and physical-mortal life and spiritual-mortal beings, it is never frustrated. It is never fearful. One who acts from Presence has no need of anger, then. They may act in ways that appear like anger, especially to other mortals,[26] but that is not the case. Their acts may even be physically destructive, very much so, but the emphasis is more like preparing the earth to receive seed, rather than situational irritation. [vii] As such, these actions are actually akin to the seed being destroyed so the tree can come forth, a way for Life to manifest again. Does that make sense to you?"

The Wanderer chuckled, remembering the anger he had felt earlier that day – or lifetime – when he had been angry with The Being for creating the desert itself. It seemed absurd now, mere paces from both the desert and The Being to have ever been frustrated with his divine Teacher.

He looked at him humbly, "So is anger just more distraction?"

"Not exactly. Anger is just another *manifestation* of one's ability to be distracted, a tool for observing distraction and potentially receiving individual instruction via the pain distraction causes in this place, in a mortal existence. Understand the difference?"

---

[26] What with Mr. Potatohead-esque "angry eyes" and all...

"I think so," The Wanderer replied. "It's like what we were talking about before. The anger is not the distraction any more than lust or any other human emotion might become so. When it appears it's just a sign that the mortal is distracted, right?"

"Yes, and nearly anything can become a distraction in mortality. Any one thing, or group of things, can distract one from the Language of the Earth and Creator. Even things that are generally regarded as desirable from a spiritual or consciousness standpoint in mortality, in excessive amounts or with an unhealthy level of attachment, can become distractions. They can even command so much mortal attention that the Language can be blocked and, as we have seen, the mortal can become lost. We were talking about the "seekers" before and some of the religious people – especially those that start religions. They can be great examples of this."

"It's funny," The Wanderer said. "I was taught at some point back in my experience to regard those that started or led religions as especially... 'righteous,' I guess."

The Being replied, "Understand: they absolutely can be especially brave and enlightened. Many of those that have had experiences and started movements that have become religions have brought change to the temporarily dominant culture that postponed the destruction of the earth for many hundreds of years. [27] In this way they served mankind and Life to a very great extent, to the utmost of their capability. But it is a condition of human mortality to be distracted from the Language of the Earth unless distraction in all its forms is recognized and stillness is embraced."

The Wanderer nodded. "OK. So, can I ask about Amy and her ability to take stillness with her? At first, she had to "get away" from strife to find it. Later, she brought it with her wherever she was, *in spite* of strife."

"Yes, exactly. What is your question?" The Being nodded approvingly.

"Well, what made her able to keep stillness within her?" The Wanderer shrugged.

The Being answered, "It was, as you sensed, more than being raised on a farm, although Amy used that early benefit to her advantage. As you observed, she found meditation early in life and recognized the feeling that came to her when she practiced as coming from stillness. Far from simply calling it a 'practice',[28]

---

[27] If The Being were talking about this earth's incarnation specifically he would mention Martin Luther and the Buddha. But he's not necessarily talking about this earth's incarnation, is he?

she actually used her sitting time as practice for dealing in a healthy way with life's situations. For instance, she saw that when her mind would wander during meditation, bringing it back was the same as not getting drawn into an angry co-worker's complaint, or a disappointing situation like sitting in traffic, or simply feeling lonely. The more she practiced, the more able she was to see which of her potential reactions to any situation came from stillness, and which did not."

The Wanderer nodded.

"Furthermore, she noticed an interesting phenomenon: the more she practiced, the more time she felt she had, in the moment, to choose an appropriate response. It was almost like an expansion of time wherein she could see and carefully consider the potential of each response before acting. Even though the time elapsed might be only seconds, because of her practice, she felt not only able to slow the stimulus/event, but to breathe Stillness into it and to carefully choose an action in response to it, and then act from that place. More often than not, this brought peace or stillness to a situation where it might not have been otherwise, or deepened stillness where it was already present."

---

[28] Note: Those who practice (verb) meditation, call the practice their "practice" (noun).

"Did time really expand for her?" The Wanderer asked.

"Actually, yes," The Being replied, "in certain moments Time was her servant, although she would never guess that. But as interesting as that may be, it's not very important. The main effect of her practice on this feeling of controlling time was not its expansion; rather it was a decrease in the number of her possible reactions. Rage, for instance, was simply no longer an option in *any* circumstance, so its absence gave room to consider potential reactions in a quantum instant on a subconscious level. Eventually, so many unconscious ways of behaving were eliminated that instead of having to consider five or six she would only have to consider one or two, and she could do that almost at her leisure. It felt like controlling time."

"But isn't it simply human nature to feel rage, or at least anger? Not to mention lust, happiness, disappointment... I mean, without emotions we would look pretty...scary, really." The Wanderer shook his head, frowning.

The Being spoke slowly, raising a finger to the sky to make his point. "Allowing human mortal nature to run humanity is what produces temporarily dominant cultures. Consider that, aside from simply wishing for more and more unique experiences and adventures, a main force driving Creative Intelligence when it chooses a spirit to inhabit in preparation for a mortal human sojourn is this: how to remain connected to Intelligence from the vantage of mortality. For non-human animals, for whom there is inherently less struggle with distraction, this is not the issue. They are driven by instinct and are given a smaller measure of "thought and decision-making potential" within the parameters of their chosen mortality. A dolphin, for instance, has slightly more of this potential than a spider. But even the most capable dolphin has hardly any of this potential compared to a human. *It's important to remember that humans are not here to be merely human.* That comes instinctually as a result of being born into a human body. Rather, humans are on earth to remember and act from a place of spirit, ultimately Intelligence, ultimately as co-Creator of their individual realities.[29]

---

[29] Modern science is beginning to understand and quantify what has been known for centuries by mystics, shaman and wise men and women from many cultures; that our realities are malleable to an extent that is almost scary. It is scary because of how little we do with the power that is inherently ours if we cared enough to learn to manipulate it, and not always for reasons of great apparent import like faith-based physical, mental and spiritual healing. For instance, Nat Young, the great 70's surfer, said once that he caught a wave in South Africa that he sincerely believes he mentally controlled. Within the parameters of modern quantum science, this is entirely plausible. Another story, told to a close friend of a trusted friend of mine, went that the man claims to have seen Nepalese monks passing a butter

"Co-creator? With …" The Wanderer interrupted.

"I believe we will address that question later. For now, let me finish," The Being said patiently. "Dolphins are here to be dolphins, spiders to be spiders, badgers to be badgers, flies to be flies. But humans… they are to see these aspects of their humanity arise and then dismiss the parts that are in conflict with Intelligence; to see the inherent rift between their own mortal nature and their true Nature. True human nature is not human at all. Ultimately, it is spirit ascended from pure Intelligence, pure potentiality and pure creativity. Humans alone are equipped to see the effects of different acts on their own lives and those of their fellow explorers. But so often…most often…they choose not to see, or, more accurately, to make choices that prevent proper seeing. They then act from human mortal nature rather than by human spiritual nature and pure Understanding. This causes failure to allow Intelligence to guide them through their felt sense, because they are too distracted to hear it."

"So, her practice was more important to her ability to be still and grounded and connected to her spirit - and ultimately her Intelligence - than anything else?" The Wanderer concluded.

---

dish at a table using nothing but mental will. That might have seemed unimportant, but then again maybe they really, *really* needed that butter.

"Absolutely, once she commenced the path to that end," The Being smiled.

"And this is so she could...what, kind of have time to make decisions when situations arose that were just part of life?" The Wanderer asked.

"It's not time, right?" The Being reiterated. "Without getting too far afield, we have established that Time has a shape, it is a conscious entity, a Being. This is how it was Amy's servant in particular instances. But that's not critical to understand right now. Amy has all the time she needs, whether she practices or not. In a more meaningful sense as it pertains to her mortal place, time is relative: she only has so much of it between stimulus and necessary response. Her practice, as you pointed out earlier, eventually... *eventually*... simply "thinned out" the number of responses that were acceptable to her spirit, and ultimately to her Intelligence. But I know you understand that the point is not "additional time." This is only a desirable by-product of the kind of life Amy lives. Of course, the point of mortality for most of humankind is to make a known connection to the Source from the mortal plane. To consistently operate from a state of connected consciousness...this is the great game."

The Wanderer looked at the rock under his feet, thinking. Shaking his head, he looked at the Being. "You say this happened eventually, but it looked like she got it right away. I mean, I know she was born with certain advantages, but her speedy advancement makes it look so seamless. How did she get so advanced so fast?"

The Being chuckled and shook his head. "Typical: another good question but drawn from an incorrect assumption."

"What assumption was incorrect this time?" The Wanderer asked, frowning.

"The assumption that she has made any advances that could even remotely be called 'speedy'".

"Well, it seemed pretty fast to me, even with parents that... were wise." The Wanderer looked questioningly at his Teacher.

"Time, as you are referring to it here, is relative, and Amy is no hummingbird. Neither are you, now." The Being looked searchingly into The Wanderers eyes.

The Wanderer paused and looked up at the sky, in thought. Suddenly looking back at The Being he exclaimed, "Oh...she's had a few chances to get it right?"

"Yes," The Being chuckled again, nodding. "Quite a few."

The Wanderer paused and frowned, considering this. "And what about Maya and her father, the businessman?" A thought had come to him. To The Wanderer, it was almost terrifying.

The Being had read his thoughts and now his eyes sparkled. "Now you're getting it. Those three have been playing together much, much longer than you can comprehend - even in your dream state. If you could see it all, you would know that many times Amy failed. And when Amy did not, many times Maya did not connect with Amy or she could not refuse the gift from her father. Other times her father didn't care that Maya did refuse it; to him she was just "spoiled". And each time the earth was affected in a different manner."

The Wanderer's eyes narrowed. "How often does this happen? How often do three people interact until they act in a way that... and is it always three, and what..."

"Please don't try to use your mind to ask this question," The Being spoke as he usually did, with a lightness that seemed like play but with serious overtones.

The Wanderer's jaw was slack. "You mean to tell me that this happens with everyone and their interaction with each other and the earth?" He paused, considering the magnitude of the concept. "It's all so...huge," was all he could say. After a pause, he asked, "So let me get this straight..."

"Again, be careful," The Being interrupted, "this is not Sunday School. Please don't get hung up on mental concepts. Instead, remember that a felt-sense is what is required. You do not have the language to describe it all. Language, even thought is far too limiting for this concept by nearly an infinite exponential factor. You are not built that way, even in a dream state. You need to understand the concept exclusively, for now, by way of a felt-sense."

The Wanderer nodded, but he couldn't help it. His face was trancelike, his eyes a thousand miles away. He spoke haltingly, not much more than a whisper. "OK... but just like my hummingbird was kind of like the centerpiece of its world and he affected it in his own small way, and then the world lived and died... just like that, the world is affected by Amy, and the world lives and dies, and Maya, and her father...and each is the center of their own world... is that somehow how it is?"

The Being looked at him without expression. "That is correct; it is *somehow* how it is. Not precisely, but as close as you will come to describing the Great Mechanism of Life on this Earth. Remember a felt-sense, please."

The Wanderer looked pale and put his hands on his knees. Looking at the rock and sand beneath his feet he continued to speak in the same halting manner. "It's so huge. Life is … huge. The Creator… so inconceivable… I, I feel so small. How can any Being keep everything this complex so… so it all works? So that it's organized?"

The Being looked compassionately at The Wanderer and placed a hand on his back, kindly and gently. Feeling the depth of his kindness and compassion, The Wanderer continued, "So, each time a person or animal lives, that being affects the earth and others. And through that being's actions another of earth's incarnations lives and dies, right? Where does it end?"

The Being looked into The Wanderer's eyes as he stood back up, speaking slowly. "Please let the concept alight and inform, rather than forcing your understanding into the concept. A hummingbird does not land on a moving hand. Stillness is required. But to answer your question, the fact is that it doesn't end. All life, from a tree frog to a blue whale, affects the earth, which is a great receptor and communicator, the Oracle of the Creator to all mortal life. Each manifestation of Life again, from the smallest to the greatest, makes its impact. Each changes the course of life on the earth within its incarnation and, hence, changes the earth. The earth lives and goes through its apparent destruction at the end of the impact of a temporarily dominant culture[30] affected in some small or great way by the choices of each being, however small.[31] In the end, each potentiality must be accounted for and the impact of every mortal choice seen – however minute and however massive."

The Wanderer shook his head, overwhelmed with the concept of a whole earth "existence" being affected by a sloth that may

---

[30] It could be argued that at any given time on Earth there is a "most-powerful" culture, and that all cultures are temporary (or have been so far). While that may be true, a culture in line with the Language would not be dominant as much as it would exist in accordance with the Earth and, hence, the Language. Cultures that exist in this way would not necessarily be temporary, unless they are destroyed by another culture. Of course history is full of stories of this nature.

[31] *HOWEVER* small... for instance, a shark may live well before mankind walks the earth, moving perfectly within the natural order of life. But his impact is still felt in the future via the impact he had on the DNA pool that he necessarily at least temporarily thinned out, the instinctual fear he strengthened in the species he hunted, the fact that he propagated a species that continues today and *does* have an impact on mankind. Sometimes we forget that eternity runs both ways from where we now stand and that each being's history radiates in ways that seem incomprehensibly small. But then we weren't the ones living in the orbit of the shark's existence. Probably.

have lived in a jungle once, or a cat in an apartment in a big city, or a wolf on the tundra, or a woman that saw him there. Seeing this struggle on the face of his pupil, The Being added, "Remember…"

"I know," The Wanderer sighed, "a 'felt sense' of the concept, not the description." After a pause, The Wanderer asked, "Where do all these earths go? Are you really telling me that one of earth's existences were… or *are*… built around my hummingbird? And that one is built around each *version* of every living thing that ever exists on the earth, and that these potentialities exist more or less simultaneously? That seems a little far-fetched."

"Far-fetched to whom, and on what basis? And although some of what you said is accurate, it is so woefully short of being complete that it may threaten the truth that has lit your soul since our conversation began. Again, this is not a religion," The Being warned.

The Wanderer nodded. "I guess I see your point. If I've learned one thing from our little conversation, it's that just because it's incomprehensible to me *in this space* doesn't mean it's not the way it is in some fashion, I guess."

"Do you remember seeing the destruction at the end of the incarnation of your hummingbird?"

"How can I forget? Is there something I missed?" The Wanderer asked, looking worried.

The Being smiled. "I'm glad you asked. We weren't done. Watch."

"Every time you say that..." Still looking a little pale, The Wanderer shook his head and gave a wan smile back.

The coolness of the vision in the lake brought some relief to the overwhelmed Wanderer. As the hue came to them from the water and flowed around them, it was a relief to him from the constant physical, mental and emotional effort that he had experienced on this day that seemed without end. There was even a smell like that of clear, cool water. He breathed easily and deeply, at complete peace while sharing this space with The Being that had patiently and wisely taught him so much, or at least tried to. He looked over at The Being. He looked familiar, but The Wanderer was certain he had never laid eyes on him before. How could he have? But still...

Just as he was about to ask The Being about his personal origin, a familiar light in the inky darkness caught his eye. Immediately the vision he had seen before of the destruction of the earth exploded into his view. Once again, he saw the deadness of the once-beautiful planet. He saw the rotting carcasses of the organisms on it, once so full of grace, life and potential. But that potential was finished forever in this space. Their spirits were gone now and the lessons learned were helping or hindering, bringing peace or further distraction to other Selves in an infinite dance that The Wanderer could barely begin to begin to begin to begin to sense and feel but never fully describe, even to himself.

As the scene unfolded in front of them, The Wanderer sensed a depth of sorrow in the very air around them, a choking feeling that felt like confusion in the face of something so shocking that it was again incomprehensible. What was shocking? Was it the scale of death? The stillness? Was it the very images themselves – the little girl clutching a stuffed toy, her small hands clenching the fake fur of the toy she had hoped would save her life? Was it the once-glorious and graceful animals frozen in their writhing, the wise old forests leveled, the wondrous cities crumbled?

No…it was more than this, and he could barely comprehend it, let alone accept it. It was that somehow this was someone's will - that there was a being for whom this was an acceptable outcome.

A thought began to form in his mind, a teaching from some lifetime once lived: a being that rejoiced in misery, that called itself the Destructor. Only something that evil, that contrary and that ill could rejoice in this, or even accept it.

Still seemingly encased in the indigo water with endless scenes of carnage parading in front of them, The Wanderer asked the Being, "Is there a devil? And did it do this?"

The Being looked at The Wanderer as if he felt the question coming before it had been asked, as the scenes continued behind him. "Are you asking me if there is an evil that is somehow equal to or greater than the Creator? Or that disrupts the peace of the Creator? Or that somehow the Creator is at war and hence, not in control?"

"I guess so," The Wanderer said meekly wishing he had not asked. "I guess I've never heard it put that way. It's just that when I saw things growing and progressing in wisdom and making changes that were good, healthy, I felt a sense of things being right, of a divine will being fulfilled. The people I saw, Maya and her father, Amy and hers, the man from Chicago...all these people were on the verge of making choices that would help themselves and many other people feel the Language. This seemed like a great good, the best thing they could do."

The Wanderer paused, looking intently at the Being, who returned his gaze calmly as the scenes continued behind him.

"You are looking for something that does not exist, and it is typical of the mortal mind," The Being said.

"What am I looking for?" The Wanderer frowned.

"Ultimately, you are looking for lasting peace in this place," he said, gesturing with his hand to the carnage behind him. "Furthermore, and possibly more importantly, you are defining peace as the absence of pain, the absence of strife and struggle. This is folly, as ridiculous as picking up a flat stone and being surprised that it has more than one side. As we spoke about, it is understood by the spirit before mortality that death and change are part of the bargain of mortal life, and that to the mortal mind it can be horrific."

"Are you saying this is the way it's supposed to be? All this pain, this destruction?" A scene of a family huddled in a modern living room in death's embrace came up behind the Being. Indicating it, The Wanderer said, raising his voice, "This is acceptable to the same Being that created the Language, that created all the stars and planets, and Time? To the same Being that created all that Order? This disorder, this sickening destruction is part of that Being's grand plan?" The Wanderer's voice was rising. "I can't believe it! Did you create this, too, just like the desert?"

The Being closed his eyes and stifled a laugh. When he opened his eyes they were locked on The Wanderers. He shook his head, appearing to wonder at the depth of misunderstanding of his pupil. Of course, he wasn't.

"Dear Wanderer," he said with real compassion, "open your eyes to the whole mechanism, not just the tiny portion you see. Is there pain in these scenes?" He paused and regarded them before speaking slowly, his face now deadly serious. "More than you can comprehend at this moment. Is this somehow omniscient will? Absolutely. Now before you respond, may I ask you a question?"

The Wanderer nodded.

"If I were to pick up the flat stone I mentioned before and labeled one side of it "Creation", what would the other side be labeled," and then smiling and raising his eyebrows playfully he added, "assuming it had another side?"

"Destruction," The Wanderer said softly, eyes cast downward.

"Destruction," The Being repeated, nodding.

"So," The Wanderer asked in frustration, "if this is Creator's will, why don't I feel the same way when I see this...this *carnage* in front of me as I did when I saw Amy's father begin to feel the

121

Language? And I never heard the Language say anything about destruction."

"You did not hear the Language say anything about destruction because you were not keyed to it in its entirety, nor could you be. You saw what was pleasing to you. I told you about Amy's failings in past existences, and those of Maya and her father, but you were not shown these things so they were only conceptual to you. But they are, and were, present failures in connection, philosophy, manner and habit, to name a few, not to mention their manner of seeing time - in a linear fashion - that we discussed earlier. Now, in order to deepen your understanding, again, by way of a felt-sense, you should know that mortals strive in a way that is separate from the way of Creator. Creator is neither alive nor dead. Creator simply *is* in a way that you will not comprehend, almost like a third potential state. Mortals call the type of existence that they have "life" and anything unlike their existence, "death". This is as it should be: their instinct is to live after the manner of their existence, the only one known to them by Creative design and by agreement before Intelligence begins to move "independently" of All That Is. Mortals are kept from most knowledge of All That Is, otherwise the Knowledge itself would become yet another distraction, much like religion can be."

"But I will remind you now that all things in a mortal plane ebb and flow. The ebb from the kind of life you enjoy is called death. There is an instinctual knowledge for a mortal that life is a condition that is desirable to maintain. Human mortals – and some nonhuman ones - add to this by feeling that there is much to experience in mortality; another reason, besides mere instinct, to live. So, the mortal in his natural state walks in defense, if not fear or dread, of death. And as death is presumably preceded by pain, he walks in fear of that, too. This innate fear of pain extends to all change, as change is a type of death and a subconscious reminder of it. It is also, quite significantly, what keeps those in power from accepting Teachers that would instruct them to change."

"So, what does that have to do with my original question about a Destructor?"

"That wasn't exactly your *original* question, was it?"

Considering this, The Wanderer replied, "Oh... my original question was how the same Being that created the Earth and the Language could approve of this level of destruction. I guess my assumption was that only a Being that was inherently evil could approve of this."

"Your....?" The Being paused.

The Wanderer closed his eyes, shaking his head at his mistake. "Assumption," he admitted.

The Being nodded. "You wonder why religion is merely a distraction for most mortals? This is a perfect illustration."

"I see," The Wanderer conceded, nodding.

The Being continued, "The answer to your original question can be found as you consider what I told you about the nature of your mortal life tempered with what you have seen in vision, both the easy and the difficult for you to regard as a mortal. And above it all, an overriding sense of something unfathomably and infinitely *more* and yet the same; as water can be solid, liquid or steam – it is all ultimately one. Creator is one. You are one with Creator. You Create."

"And that makes the destruction ok?"

The Being closed his eyes briefly and shook his head. "The destruction simply *is*. It is the other side of the same stone; the ice to the water to the steam, a different form." Looking at the rock beneath his feet before continuing, he said, "As I mentioned before, as a mortal, it is in your nature to strive. You strive to preserve life, which is what all mortals do. But what happens to an *unconscious* human is also fear; the fear of death and, by implication, the fear of change. It is in this fear trio that man meets his greatest challenge. Enmeshed in the nature of Life with its innate chaos, the man strives not only to preserve his life, but also for a respite from striving. He calls this respite 'peace', but true peace can only be had by facing and embracing death, pain and change, not hiding from them."

"That seems contradictory," The Wanderer noted, processing, "but it's like the teaching that a seed has to die before it can become a tree? It's all part of the process, all sacred, all…good?"

"Exactly. And that fear gets increasingly intense the more insulated the human is from Nature, because they've insulated themselves from the healthful process of change, or death," The Being replied.

He let that sink in and then added, "In latter temporarily dominant cultures, the vast majority of participants in human mortality search for peace in noise, in distraction, anything to avoid facing this Trio. So, it's all in where one chooses to put the effort. Just as the drowning man wishes to breathe but will find no satisfaction by breathing in water, trying to find peace in distraction will result in destruction, both cultural and personal. So, finding and remembering the Language is an acceptable effort, as it also entails an acceptance of Life and a facing of death in all its forms. Accept the destruction as a part of a larger context of Life even as you strive to create more room for life and more time before the destruction of each moment, whatever its form. Each moment simply is. Peace, as it truly is, can be glimpsed in small *moments* for mortals by understanding this with their hearts."

"So, acceptance of the process and characteristics of Life, even the wild part of it, is important then, right? And the... "is-ness" or the "being-ness"... of each moment, too, I guess? " The Wanderer asked.

"Excellently put, yes. Destruction, as pain, is a great teacher. Some indigenous spiritual paths lionize the image of the destructor as one who teaches through painful experience, even through deception. Iktomi the Trickster of the Sioux and the destructive portion of the Hindu god Shiva are fine examples of this, but by no means the only ones."

There was a pause, as both looked towards the lake.

"Something just occurred to me," The Wanderer said slowly. "We're been talking about how the earth speaks a sacred language, like it's an oracle, right?"

"Yes…" The Being replied, knowing an insightful question was about to be asked.

"What about our bodies?" The Wanderer asked.

The Being beamed but said nothing.

Encouraged, The Wanderer continued. "The earth is an oracle for us, speaking the Language through Stillness that we know but have forgotten through distraction. But it seems that our Intelligences would want something… even closer, if that's the right word?" The Wanderer paused, frowning, looking across the great, round lake at the red rocks that seemed like another lifetime away."

He let that thought take wing before continuing. "If All That Is wanted to allow us to hear the Voice at any and all times, wouldn't our spirits want to be in a…a *machine* that was a type of radio itself? It seems like our spirits would want to be in a mechanism for travel in this foreign place that allowed continuous, direct communication with the Language as well as information about the machine itself… is that what our bodies do?"

The Being laughed, nodding. "Yes, in essence that's it, Wanderer. Stillness is the key and the Language is the same."

"Is the message the same no matter if it comes through the Earth or the body?"

"That's not quite the right question as it again contains an incorrect assumption. All messages to mortal individuals *must* come through the body, and most come from the oracle of the Earth itself. But aside from this, the answer is 'yes' but with different emphasis. The Earth speaks primarily of things on a macro scale, of all Life. The body is a vehicle of human mortality, so messages from the Earth may have particular validity to the individual, but not necessarily. One thing to note is that the body itself is generally concerned with the spirit's ability to receive messages. The health of the body can be a gauge of the spirit's ability to receive communications, among many other things. But to answer your question, Earth messages and body messages will never contradict, as they are from the same source."

"The body is really a receiver of messages, then, right?" The Wanderer asked. "Wow... so even physical health has a spiritual component to it?"

"Oh, yes! The spirit, hence Intelligence, cannot interact in the physical plane without it, and all things being equal, a healthy body will receive messages more effectively than an unhealthy one. Conversely, not all messages are healthy to receive. The quality of the messages that the spirit allows affect the health of the body as well as the spirit's ability to hear more."

"Some messages from the Earth are harmful?" The Wanderer frowned.

The Being shook his head. "No, of course not. They are always in line with Life and Intelligence. But mortal-to-mortal communication also comes from energy and is made of energy. What a mortal chooses to ingest *from other mortals* can affect his ability to hear messages made of purer material."

"OK, I get that. What and whom the mortal chooses to surround himself with, on an energetic level, will affect his own energy. But if the spirit is like – I don't know – the child of the Intelligence, why would it ever choose messages that affect its ability to hear?"

"Why would a young child ever disobey its parent, a being vastly wiser than they? While this is not a perfect example, it is similar. Sometimes a spirit needs to experience something that appears to be unwise, that creates individual or even cultural discord. It is then the mortal's challenge to wrest control from the body and mind and bring both back into more typical line with spirit and Intelligence. Sometimes this is the way it was ordained to be; to allow the spirit to let go of the wheel a while simply for the experience of regaining control. Remember the example of Shiva; destruction is, at times, the best option for growth. At other times the spirit is simply unwise. After all, this is a land that is foreign and there are many unfamiliar situations for even the wisest, oldest spirit-wanderer. But then this is the whole point. Getting in and then out of situations unique to this land gives the spirit and Intelligence what it has and desires: strength and depth, experience and wisdom. At other times the embodied spirit may make a choice that ensnares it and addiction ensues. The spirit becomes identified with the drama that the body allows in this place by the very nature of a mortal sojourn, except it is now exacerbated by addiction. As it is not in the spirit's nature to be confined, this extra confinement can cause great destruction on the earth, especially when many embodied spirits have become addicted. Addiction to one thing or another is the most common state in the latter end of temporarily dominant cultures. It becomes an almost universal addiction to distraction, with its attendant destruction. And most don't even know they're addicted."

The Wanderer considered this and asked, "But what about old age? People get old and their bodies break down, right? That's not because the spirits have let in weak or substandard messages, is it? Distraction isn't the issue there."

"Well, yes and no. Aside from the fact that mortal bodies are not created to be perpetually self-sustaining, aging is a function of two things. First, there is an expectation that old age and death will happen at a generally predictable time. Simply put, a child asks its parent when it will die and the child identifies with the answer and her own observations over time. In other words, it is a type of mortal body conditioning. Secondly, it is as you alluded: the condition of mortal old age is an accepted condition, as accepted as the presence of potential traps and snares in mortality. Yes, a body sickened by illness – whether caused by age or not – is often less attentive to the finer communications of the Language. After all, sickness of the body can itself become a distraction, or the nature of the sickness dims the ability to hear. In this instance it has nothing to do with the voices to which the mortal has listened. But you will also find those that fairly glow from within the closer to death they become. These are those that are not distracted by illness but have rather been strengthened by it. They have transcended the mortal plane, and they shine."

Looking down at the vision of the dead earth with its heaps of bodies and destruction, The Wanderer asked, "And what about this? You were going to show me where this earth went, the one that my hummingbird had lived upon?"

Once again, The Being exclaimed joyfully, "Watch!"

The earth turned sleepily as the two looked on. One thing that had changed since the final wars on earth was the weather. Huge, incessant windstorms, inconceivable to mankind when he was on the earth, swept it with force. It was common to see massive objects flying through the air high into the atmosphere. On occasion a twisted truck might fly by, or a bent and broken boat or even a small ship.

Still, a sudden massive movement near the horizon caught The Wanderers eye. But it wasn't the movement itself. Again, wind was ever-present. It was the direction. The direction was straight up and the size of what lifted from the earth was huge. Something massive and incredibly fast had launched itself from the earth straight into the sky, held aloft by the wind high to nearly to the edge of the earth's atmosphere before breaking up into what looked like a cloud in the distance.

"What was that?" The Wanderer asked. But The Being stared straight ahead, the corners of his mouth turned slightly upwards as more movement, massive and unexpected, turned The Wanderers head back again.

As he did so, The Wanderer saw what he had missed before: deserts of sand suddenly shooting up from where they sat, filling the sky and obscuring the earth with dust and debris. The sand came from the bottoms of all the oceans, from forests and mountains, from steppes and savannahs, from river bottoms and jungles. It appeared to The Wanderer that sand from all over the earth - a great portion of all of it upon the spinning planet - was suddenly immune to gravity. Borne by hurricane winds the world over, it stayed aloft, shrouding the planet in an otherworldly darkness. Very little sunlight at all penetrated the cloud of sand, as thick as it was.

Just as The Wanderer was about to ask The Being about this unimaginable oddity, he saw simultaneous fires start in many of the unfathomably large piles of dead timber and detritus that remained on the earth. The timber, dry as bleached bones under previously incessant sun and wind simply started to smoke, and then tentative flames appeared. The fires spread quickly on their own, stoked by the howling winds.

As the heat intensified, trees exploded and streams, rivers and, eventually, seas were licked dry. Buildings, structurally weakened by the heat, crumbled. The very air itself seemed aflame as the fire continued to intensify. Diminished light from the sun shrouded the earth which was continually blanketed by the hovering atmospheric deserts. The fire was like a new and lonely life form, and now the main source of light for the planet.

After what seemed like decades of intense burning on the earth and in the sky itself (during which time the desert sands remained aloft), the great, angry fire died down, eventually running out of consistent fuel. The Wanderer could see, here and there, part of the evidence of the former inhabitants' civilization, if it could be called that (for The Wanderer had observed what a misnomer the term "civilization" that had been for this species before their self-destruction). He could see the weakened and twisted skeletons of a few remaining skyscrapers and ships, glowing waste dumps and other substantial trash heaps.

The scene paused, and The Wanderer looked at The Being for meaning. Their eyes met, and The Being smiled. "Now, watch this!"

The Wanderer smiled back tentatively and, following the eyes of the Being, looked down at the Earth in wonder.

To his amazement, everything that was left upon the earth that had been charred, which was everything that could be seen by The Wanderer, began to be peeled back like the outside of a burnt marshmallow, gathering at one point on the lonely planet before sinking into its depths. Dark, charred matter ran toward one point as steel is drawn toward a magnet, disappearing like water down a drain into the middle of the earth. As he watched this in wonder, another image that seemed to illustrate deeper what he was seeing also went through The Wanderers mind; an experience that seemed oddly familiar.

A young boy stood bending over in the clearing of a dense, lush, jungle. The Wanderer could see him plainly. His skin was brown and exposed. He wore only the skin of an animal around his waist. A small knife with a handle of bone hung from a belt that appeared to be made of hair. The boy's own long hair obscured his face as he bent over. The jungle itself had been briefly filled with the sounds of laughing boys his age, but the laughter had crashed away through the jungle and The Wanderer could now only hear the boy making sounds like he was in pain. He could see blood dripping off the boy's arm onto the moist earth. Stopping the sounds of anguish, the boy reached down and picked up something that looked like another leaf off the forest floor. Standing now, his long hair partially obscuring his face and cascading down his back, the boy examined what he held: a scab, newly torn from his arm while in the act of play. The boy looked at it, and then at his bleeding arm. He wiped away the blood from the newly opened wound with his other forearm and watched as it refilled with new blood like a puddle over rain-saturated earth refills after the water has been splashed out. The boy blew on the wound, bringing more pain and then relief at almost the same time. The Wanderer saw the boy look in the direction his companions had gone, into the walled jungle

around him, and then at the scab he held in his dirty fingers. The
boy balled up the scab, threw it on the ground and ran in the
direction of his friends, his arm dripping blood, a smile on his
face.

The Wanderer also smiled, a sense of pride filling him. He knew this boy, nearly remembered being this boy, somehow. Had he been? He felt he knew him so well. But as The Wanderer watched him run off into the jungle, his attention turned in hyper-detail to the scab the boy had thrown on the ground. Blood moist, it had balled easily and now sat plainly on a leaf, a tiny planet in a jungle ocean of green and brown.

Why had this vision appeared now?

His vision lifted from the scab on the ground to the jungle, to the continent, to the earth below him as it presently was. He saw the spinning debris surrounding the earth in a dark hug. The charred remains of the outer planet below him had apparently disappeared, leaving glowing molten rock oozing upwards, blood red out of the remaining earth's crust.

Had it all gone under the earth, into its center? Had all the evidence of collective humanity really slid off the face of the earth and sunk into a great hole within it, like a child pulls the charred skin of a marshmallow off it to reveal a portion that has been untouched?

He was about to comment on this, when he suddenly saw something rocket straight up from the very place into which the earth's crust had disappeared. It spit into the middle of the desert detritus that was still held aloft by the swirling, intense winds. It was tiny but amazingly bright, as bright as the sun, showing through all the swirling sand. He watched this tiny point mix and shine through the swirl, sometimes bright and sometimes dim. He knew what he was seeing was important, but he didn't know why.

Before he could ask The Being about the tiny light, his attention turned again to the earth below him. It appeared to begin to turn inside out! It was not exactly what happened, but it is what went through The Wanderers mind. Violent volcanic eruptions covered the planet, looking like destruction and creation at the same time, and the thought of the flat stone, of Shiva and even of Johnson Mays' plow went through his mind. The eruptions went on for a thousand years, bathing most of the earth in their fiery glow. Ancient mountains sunk into the earth and new ones arose, borne of earthquake and fire, as if the earth were giving birth to itself. He saw the rage diminish over many years but the wind and the swirling deserts of sand were ever above. Then, all at once, the wind began to decrease in intensity and the deserts of sand began to fall, blanketing the earth, smothering the cooling lava.

The Wanderer and The Being were back, standing on the rock at the edge of the desert, overlooking the sparkling blue, circular lake.

"What did I just see?" The Wanderer asked in a whisper to the Being, who stood in an attitude of love that had never been felt by The Wanderer before.

"Look at your feet. Do you see that sparkling grain of sand by your right toe?"

The Wanderer chuckled before looking downward. "I'm looking for a grain of sand in a desert?" he said smiling wryly as he looked down. But when he saw it his smile faded. At his feet was a sparkling grain of sand poised on the very rock upon which he stood. Other than the slightly different color of the grain of sand, which he would not have noticed if The Being had not called it to his attention, it looked similar to the sand that made up the desert that filled his vision to the horizon on all sides. He got down on his hands and knees to get a better look.

"You just saw the destruction of the world that you, as a bird, lived upon.

"Yes, I understand that," The Wanderer replied, and then froze, paralyzed by the enormity of the seed of a thought.

The Being squatted next to The Wanderer and picked up the grain of sand that The Wanderer had been studying and stood up. The Wanderer sat where he was and stared at the vacant space where the grain had been, still amazed at the thoughts whirling through his spinning mind. The Being held the grain of sand on the tip of his finger and looked past it at the back of the head of the crouching Wanderer. "This is it," he said.

The Wanderer knew what he was talking about but it was too incredible to comprehend. Still on the ground he looked up and asked, "This is what?"

"This is what you might call the "skin"[32] of the world that you just saw. It's what was removed after the destruction of the world, condensed by the earth itself, into this."

The Wanderer said nothing. He just blinked, dumbfounded.

The Being smiled and continued. "And that's not even what's interesting."

---

[32] ...or scab...

"It's not? Then what's interesting? I mean, I think it was *kind of* interesting that the whole surface of the earth was condensed into a grain of sand… I mean, that's kind of interesting, to me," The Wanderer deadpanned. Inside he felt a sense of wonder infused with intense happiness that acted as the yin to wonder's yang.

"The hummingbird was your first incarnation," The Being replied. "By the way, that was a lot to take in for a first incarnation; most Intelligences take on something like an amoeba or bacteria first. You pulled it off well."

The Wanderer considered this, then pointed at the seemingly eternal dunes and spoke in a whisper, "And is some of that sand out there Maya's? And Amy's? And Maya's fathers'?"

"Yes, it is" The Being answered. "But I still didn't answer your question. In fact, I can't. For this final concept, you need only to look from where you came, and let what comes to you inform you."

The Wanderer looked past the lake and the red rock, still visible in the shimmering distance. He saw sand, an endless desert. An unspoken sense of the enormity of Life settled on his soul lightly, like a tiny hummingbird.

The Being reached down towards the sitting Wanderer, the grain of sand perched on his finger. Sensing the movement above his head, The Wanderer looked up into the Being's radiant face and reached his own hand up. The Being tipped his finger containing the grain of sand, pressing it onto The Wanderers'.

Bringing the grain of sand to his eyes, The Wanderer felt light, at peace. He could not comprehend with his mind what had been presented, but a sense of "rightness" about this inability settled over him like a blanket. He felt he held his home in his very hand, but he also felt at home where he was standing, overlooking the circular lake. In some part of his spirit, just under the words to describe it, he knew he was at home in all places at once.

This sub-mental idea brought with it a sun-kissed sense of his relation to all of Life in her trillion forms. This was precious to him, sending a presence that he recognized as Stillness coursing through his very mortality. He looked out towards the vast desert at a sandstorm blowing through the desert near the horizon; the same sand that filtered sunlight and made incredible sunsets and sunrises, sand that nearly obscured the sun and moon at times.

"Is all sand…?"

The Being looked at The Wanderer. "Not all, but more than you would imagine."

The Wanderer, still sitting, looked into the face of the Being. He looked like himself. His eyes, the kindest and wisest he could ever imagine, burned like twin suns.

Epilogue

The concepts presented to my mind while witnessing the interaction between The Wanderer and The Being are, of course, too much for my mind to comprehend. I was presented with an idea that nearly every grain of sand I see is somehow connected to choices made by individuals or groups of individuals; grains that are the result of physical manifestations of almost infinite potentialities over an incomprehensible length of time.

Just now a woman walked out of the coffee shop where I am sitting. She closed the door and then, seeing a woman about to reach for the handle, smiled and opened it for her. Is opening that door enough of an action, enough of a choice, to affect the rest of her life in some way? What about the woman for whom the door was opened? What choices will she make because the door was opened for her? Did it have any effect at all, or will she walk slightly differently today because of that action? How will her affected choices affect others'? And is there a Being that somehow keeps track of all the potentialities and collapsed waves of potential we experience from day to day?

I suspect there is, in some form.

The group that sits at my table is having an animated discussion. For how many lives have they done this? Will anything of note come of it? Who determines what is "of note"? Or did they just meet for the first time (in this life) in this coffee shop?

The fact is, it's impossible to fully comprehend a Being that could create a system as complex as that which I have attempted to describe in this work. Furthermore, I suspect that what our spirits experience in reality is far more glorious and complex than that which could ever be described in this place. In other words, a "felt sense" is the only way to begin to begin to begin to comprehend *anything* about the Creator.

Just as there are no words to describe the Mechanism, there are no words to adequately describe the Mechanic.

Instead, we should concentrate less on the stories that at one time attempted to do this impossible task, generally through religion and even science. We should instead concentrate on honoring all life, as it is certain the Creator of it does, and let what comes to us alight as a gentle hummingbird and inform our thirsty hearts.

May we simply pause and consider.

[i] The Central Oregon mystic and dear personal friend, Jeb Barton, introduced the concept of a "felt sense" to me. He describes it as I have attempted to do so here; as a fully developed idea that is simply best understood without words, even inner chatter. The trick is to sit in stillness with the tiniest particle of the concept and let the rest of it inform the soul, but without words. Of course, with a mind like mine, making it sit still takes practice, and not just meditation. In our conversations, Jeb has been generous enough to lend me some phrases he has collected or noted from different mystical disciplines from around the world. Here are a few: "Creating and transcending itself simultaneously;" "nothing is as it appears, nor is it otherwise;" "beyond timelessness;" and maybe the most directly informing in this case, "perception without images." It is in the space in our understanding between the apparent contradictions inherent in these statements that the "felt-sense" comes into play. Without a sense of stillness, the statements appear to be nonsensical. But if we sit with them and let them inform us, we open ourselves to instruction via a deeper means of perception, understanding and communication than we usually enjoy through our common language. Indeed, common language, as I have attempted to illustrate in this book, is of finite use for subjects in the field of ontology (simply put, the study of the nature of reality).

Another individual, the phenomenologist Maurice Merleau-Ponty (1908-1961) described in his book, *Phenomenology of Perception* the experience of standing in the dark as one which can point to a sense of depth, which is really what we are talking about.

"We will not necessarily find an experience of pure depth in every experience of darkness. This is because the experience of pure depth is a *pre-perceptual* experience. It is not something we see, or hear, or touch in the darkness that ushers us into an experience of pure depth. *Rather, the experience of pure depth is revealed when our perceptual experience is momentarily confounded and confused."* (Emphasis added).

It may seem odd that sitting in the dark and/or considering seemingly nonsensical and contradictory sentences would be practices that would bring one a greater understanding of things unseen and unable to be articulated, and they may not work for everyone. The reasons for this are spoken about by The Being and The Wanderer throughout the story. But it has certainly proven true that the human mind is capable of inventing all kinds of "truth" that later end up being anything but. Whether the practice of setting aside the mind to bring us to concepts more in line with reality has any practicality is up to each person to decide.

ii In 2006 I read an article that had a large part in changing my life. It was written by a female explorer named Kira Salak for the magazine, "National Geographic Adventure." In it she describes her second trip to Peru to participate in an ayhuasca ceremony with a "shaman" (in quotations because I am uncertain about how authentic this man is as such. But I will say that he apparently provided a space that worked powerfully for Ms. Salak). In her experience, she met several of her "other selves", which appeared to exist simultaneously. This rang true for me. Again, the fact that it rang true to me is unimportant, even to myself. I am not attached to "this is how it is", but I do *suspect* that this is *somehow* as it *may* be. The facts about what she was shown are ultimately unimportant unless they are shown to us directly. The felt sense is far more interesting. It is the difference between giving attention to the finite snowflakes to the exclusion of the infinite space between them.

iii That might be truer of spirits immersed in a culture that is dedicated to distraction.

iv Note: the teacher receives truth and wants to share. This is human nature in two ways. First, in a healthy way it is in accordance with Intelligence to wish to spread wisdom, to make life easier for others, to bring people along, to decrease suffering in the world. This is a beautiful and appropriate response from someone who has found something beautiful. The second way can be fraught with ego. As it often occurs, he wishes to be seen as someone who knows more than another. In either case he aligns with people that presumably have the same understanding of the basics as he does, or that want to know them. He teaches the basics to the ones lacking in understanding and imparts truth to the ones that are "already there". The issue is that the Teacher never fully knows what his students really need. The so-called godless woman may be far more advanced in spiritual matters than the spiritually intellectual. It is up to the spirit of each man to receive what he can. The problem occurs when the Teacher assumes he knows who to teach; he may say things that even a spiritually advanced man's mind gets hold of to his own detriment. This is because while he may appear to be spiritually advanced, he may have built the foundation of that spirituality on a basis that needs structural support, if not a complete rebuild. We are talking ultimately about spiritual concepts that have to be understood before words are put to them, even the words of the mind, because words never do a spiritual concept justice. Spiritual truth is ultimately communicated and understood without words, at the perfect speed when received properly, and are discerned by the spirit and Giver of the Truth only.

[v] Most "medicine men" of the Lakota Sioux are called "heyoka", meaning they do things contrary to standard ways of being. There may be many reasons for this, but I find it significant that their holiest men are called to do things "backward".

[vi] At this point a memory in explicit detail came to The Wanderer. Many times during his conversation with The Being, The Wanderer had what are often known in spiritual circles as "downloads": spiritual communications that are far more than mere thoughts. As one might imagine, a conversation with a Being of this nature would be full of them. At this point in the conversation, what flashed in the mind of The Wanderer was an event that occurred early in his childhood. More than a memory – as all communication in this dream was more complete than any he had experienced in mortality – he felt transported to the time and place I am about to describe.

I found myself standing in my second grade classroom. Mrs. Spelbrink was at the front of the class at her desk. All the children were hard at work – except Joey Runk, who had just crammed a full sheet of paper into his mouth, presumably to make a spitwad. I comprehended that the children were in the middle of an "art hour". Moving through the class like a ghost, I came up behind a child that looked especially familiar. He was like home to me. With an intense burst of nostalgia, I realized it was myself as a boy. His head was down, body hunched over a piece of paper that had his full attention. As he straightened his back to get a fuller perspective on his work, I looked into his face. I saw his innocence, his sense of humor, his purity, his kindness - all so evident to an extent he could never comprehend at this moment. It took a few moments for me to look away from his beautiful brown eyes to see at what he was smiling. It was a picture into which he had put all his effort, and it was evident that he was proud of it. My consciousness rotated around him so I could look over his shoulder at his creation. If I had breath in this space, I would have drawn it in sharply. It was a picture of a hummingbird in full Crayola regalia. I comprehended his feeling as he gazed at it. Just as I felt at home being in his small orbit, so he felt a similar home-being while he looked at his creation that day. I remember that it graced my/his bedroom wall for many years.

[vii] Shiva, the destroyer. Hindu people and many indigenous cultures throughout earth's incarnation have/have had an idea of the important nature of destruction before birth/rebirth.

Made in the
USA
Monee, IL